Understanding Jesus Today

JESUS ACCORDING TO PAUL

Understanding Jesus Today

Edited by Howard Clark Kee

Growing interest in the historical Jesus can be frustrated by diverse and conflicting claims about what he said and did. This series brings together in accessible form the conclusions of an international team of distinguished scholars regarding various important aspects of Jesus' teaching. All of the authors have extensively analyzed the biblical and contextual evidence about who Jesus was and what he taught, and they summarize their findings here in easily readable and stimulating discussions. Each book includes an appendix of questions for further thought and recommendations for further reading on the topic covered.

Other Books in the Series

Howard Clark Kee, *What Can We Know About Jesus?*
Pheme Perkins, *Jesus as Teacher*
David Tiede, *Jesus and the Future*
John Riches, *The World of Jesus: First-Century Judaism in Crisis*
James D. G. Dunn, *Jesus' Call to Discipleship*

Jesus According to Paul

VICTOR PAUL FURNISH

University Distinguished Professor of New Testament,
Perkins School of Theology,
Southern Methodist University

Published by the Press Syndicate of the University of Cambridge
The Pitt Building, Trumpington Street, Cambridge CB2 1RP
40 West 20th Street, New York, NY 10011–4211, USA
10 Stamford Road, Oakleigh, Melbourne 3166, Australia

First published 1993

Printed in Great Britain at the University Press, Cambridge

A catalogue record for this book is available from the British Library

Library of Congress cataloguing in publication data

Furnish, Victor Paul.
Jesus According to Paul / Victor Paul Furnish.
        p.   cm. – (Understanding Jesus today)
Includes bibliographical references and index.
ISBN 0 521 45193 0 (hardback) – ISBN 0 521 45824 2 (paperback)
1. Jesus Christ – History of doctrines – Early church, ca. 30–600.
2. Paul, the Apostle, Saint – Contributions in Christology.
3. Bible. N.T. Epistles of Paul – Criticism, interpretation, etc.
I. Title. II. Series.
BT198.F95 1993
232′.09′015–dc20   93–10221   CIP

ISBN 0 521 45193 0 hardback
ISBN 0 521 45824 2 paperback

CE

*To the congregation of the
Northaven United Methodist Church, Dallas
– a community of faith seriously committed to
understanding Jesus today.*

Contents

Chapter 1

From Jesus to Paul

Introduction

Jesus and Paul are the two most imposing figures to emerge from the pages of the New Testament, although for very different reasons. On the one hand, Jesus is the *subject* of every New Testament writing. In each of them, Jesus is affirmed and celebrated as the one in whom life is given and through whom it is constantly renewed and enriched. On the other hand, Paul is the *author* of more New Testament writings than any other person – and of the earliest. In addition, he is the subject of much of the Book of Acts. And when it comes to plain historical facts, we know more about Paul than about anyone else in the early church. Indeed, we know more by far about his message and mission than about Jesus' own earthly life or teaching.

It is often forgotten that Paul, whom the church came to regard as the greatest apostle of Christ, had not been one of the disciples of the earthly Jesus. Had he, in fact, even known Jesus, or even seen him? Had he ever heard Jesus teach or watched him heal? Had he ever observed him in conversation with his disciples or in dialogue with his opponents? There is no indication of this in the Gospels, where Paul is not even named, nor in the Book of Acts, where we meet him first as an opponent of the church in Jerusalem.

After Good Friday: The Church in Jerusalem

From the stories told about Jesus in the Gospels, we gain the impression that anyone who heard his teaching and observed his actions came away with a definite opinion about him. Some, even if not many, eagerly embraced his message and became devoted followers. Other rejected him as a blasphemer. For the majority, perhaps, initial curiosity would have given way eventually to a mixture of fascination and puzzlement. It is not likely that anyone who encountered him soon forgot what they had seen him doing or heard him saying. Moreover, people would have exchanged their impressions of him, whether good or bad, and doubtless would have spoken about him to those who had never been in his presence. This, at least, is what the Gospel narratives concerning Jesus' ministry suggest.

The Gospels also provide rather extended accounts of Jesus's last days and hours. We see him journeying to Jerusalem for Passover. We overhear the farewell conversations with his disciples during his last meal with them. We witness the somber events in Gethsemane, the subsequent judicial proceedings, and finally Jesus' crucifixion and burial.

The Gospels, however, provide barely a hint of how the ordinary people of Jerusalem – as distinct from the religious officials – responded to Jesus' death. We can only imagine. The populace in general probably would have been curious about why and how he had been executed. His opponents, presumably, would have felt vindicated, even relieved. His closest followers were doubtless left stunned, especially by the manner of his death – an ugly, Roman-style crucifixion. More than likely, they were fearful about their own safety.

At the very least, the disciples' experiences with Jesus and their expectations about the future must suddenly have been thrown open to question. One remark in a story in the Gospel of Luke gives some inkling of this. On the third day after the crucifixion, two of Jesus' followers are talking about what has happened as they walk along the road to the village of Emmaus. When a stranger falls in with them and asks about their conversation, he is told: "We had hoped that [Jesus] was the one to redeem Israel" (Luke 24:21). They "*had* hoped" for so much! Of course, when the curious stranger is revealed to be Jesus himself, resurrected from the dead, the despair and disillusionment of these perplexed and grieving followers gives way to faith, and the church is born.

We are dependent almost entirely on the Book of Acts for what knowledge we have of the earliest church in Jerusalem. According to Acts, it was a group of "about one hundred twenty persons" (1:15), the core of which consisted of Jesus' eleven loyal disciples (1:13). To these eleven a twelfth was soon added, replacing Judas (1:15–26). We are informed that this circle also included some women (not named), as well as Mary the mother of Jesus and Jesus' brothers (1:14).

The leadership of this congregation seems to have been at first in the hands of Peter (also known as Cephas), with whom John (a son of Zebedee) is often closely associated (Acts 3:1–11, 4:13–21; 8:14–17). Later, James, "the Just," a brother of Jesus (not to be confused with James the apostle, John's brother), comes to play at least as prominent a role (see especially, Acts 15:12–21). The special status of Peter, John, and James is also attested by Paul, who refers to them as the reputed "pillars" of the Jerusalem church (Gal 2:9). According to Acts, other important Jerusalem Christians were Barnabas (first mentioned in 4:36), John Mark (first mentioned in 12:21), Silas (first mentioned in 15:22), and a committee of seven "deacons" with Greek names (6:5). Among the latter were Philip "the evangelist" (see especially, 8:4–40) and Stephen, whose martyrdom and burial are described in 7:54–8:2). Of these other notables, only two are mentioned by Paul in his letters, Barnabas (for example 1 Cor 9:6; Gal 2:1) and Silas (evidently the "Silvanus" who is named, for example, in 2 Cor 1:19).

Paul himself is introduced to us in Acts as the "young man" Saul (his Aramaic name) who looked on approvingly as Stephen was martyred (7:58–8:1). After the account of Saul's conversion to the gospel (9:1–19), Acts will refer to him by his Roman name, Paul (13:9 and following). But we are told that before his conversion, Saul was actively engaged in persecuting the church (8:3; 9:1–2). What do we know about this man and, especially, about his relationship to Jesus and to the earliest Christian community in Jerusalem?

Paul the Pharisee

Acts is not a "church history" in the modern sense. It was not written in order to provide a report of the who, what, when, and where of the church's earliest years. Rather, its author has given us the "history of salvation" – that is, an account of how he understands *God* to have been working *through* the church. According to Acts, God's Spirit had empowered the earliest Christian generation to bear witness to their Lord, and their witness had been part of God's eternal plan for salvation. This was also the author's interest when he wrote of Paul, whose life and career he presented as vital components of salvation history. In Acts we have been offered a portrait of Paul painted in bold strokes and vivid colors. Like any good portrait it represents the artist's own conception and interpretation of the subject. For this reason, however, if we want something more like "biographical" information about Paul, we have to rely mainly on the apostle's own writings.

Paul specifically identifies himself as an ethnic Jew: "a Hebrew born of Hebrews," of Benjamin's tribe (Phil 3:5), an "Israelite" descended from Abraham (2 Cor 11:22; see also Rom 9:3–5). That he had been ritually "circumcised on the eighth day" after his birth suggests that he was the son of devout parents. He was, however, born outside of Palestine (a Jew of the Diaspora), probably in the latter years of the reign of Augustus, who died in A.D. 14. Paul's letters are written in Greek, which was apparently his first language, and he even read and quoted from a Greek version of the Jewish Scriptures. It is altogether possible that Acts (22:3) is correct in identifying his as a native of Tarsus in Asia Minor, which was an important center of Hellenistic culture.

Paul himself says that he had been "a Pharisee" as regards the law of Moses (Phil 3:5; see also Acts 23:6; 26:5). We know that Pharisaism was a lay movement, although it is unclear whether it had any kind of organizational structure. We also know that Pharisees were committed to a strict observance of the law, and that they were therefore diligent in their study of it. The Pharisees believed in a future resurrection of the dead, a final judgment, and an afterlife. Because these doctrines could not be derived from the Jewish Scriptures they were rejected by the Sadducees (another Jewish group, many members of which were priests in the temple at Jerusalem). Unlike the Sadducees, the Pharisees were guided not only by Scripture but also by unwritten traditions, the so-called "oral law." It may be this to which Paul refers when he writes of the intense devotion he once had to "the traditions" of his Jewish heritage (Gal 1:14).

How Paul learned these traditions is uncertain. We do not even know whether the Pharisees of his day had any formal training. Thus, although the Paul of Acts says that he had been tutored in the law by the noted Jerusalem teacher, Gamaliel (22:3), the apostle's own letters are silent on the point. First, he indicates that he had been an absolutely devout adherent of Pharisaism (Gal 1:14), "as to righteousness under the law, blameless" (Phil 3:6). Second, he is quite open about the fact that his commitment to the law of Moses had led him to become a determined persecutor of the church (Gal 1:13, 23; 1 Cor 15:9; Phil 3:6).

Paul the Persecutor

The Portrayal in Acts

The author of Acts depicts Paul the Pharisee as having ruthlessly and singlemindedly persecuted the Christians of Jerusalem. He had dragged Christian men and women out of their synagogues and even out of their own homes, beating them and taking them off to prison (8:3; 22:4, 19; 26:10–11). He had been in favor of putting them to death (26:10), just as he had approved and abetted the stoning of Stephen (8:1; 22:20). He was feared by Christians as far away as Damascus (9:13–14, 21), and he had even set out for that city in order to continue his evil work (9:1–2, 21; 26:11). Although many of the details of this portrayal are historically dubious, within Acts it effectively heightens the drama of Paul's own later espousal of the very gospel that he had once so strenuously opposed.

Paul's Own References

What we learn from Paul himself about this period of his life is more historically credible. In one letter, looking back, he notes the "zeal" which had moved him to persecute the church (Phil 3:6). In another letter he says that this made him "unfit" to be an apostle, so he is able to fulfill his office only "by the grace of God" (1 Cor 15:10).

Paul himself never indicates where he carried on his activities against the church, although some believe that a remark in Gal 1:22–23 provides a clue. There he quotes a report circulating among the Judean Christians: "The one who formerly was persecuting us is now proclaiming the faith he once tried to destroy." If the "us" in this statement includes the Judean Christians themselves, the passage confirms the location portrayed in Acts – that is, Jerusalem and its environs. This is unlikely, however, given Paul's main point in Gal 1:22–23. He claims that even after his conversion and first meeting with Peter (and James) in Jerusalem, he was "*still unknown by sight* to the churches of Judea that are in Christ" (v. 22), and that "they *only heard* it said, 'The one who formerly was persecuting us . . .'" etc.

Paul is also silent concerning the means by which he had "tried to destroy" the faith. It was perhaps by flogging and imprisonment, since those were the prescribed Jewish methods of punishment in his day. However, he would have had to administer these according to due process, and not (as in Acts) singlehandedly, or as one driven by a blinding rage.

In this connection, it is easy to be misled by a remark in Gal 1:13, often mistranslated. Here Paul is not saying that he had once persecuted the church of God "*violently*" (NRSV), or "*savagely*" (REB). The phrase in question is best translated "intensely" or "superlatively." Given the context (see v. 14), it seems clear that he is representing himself as having persecuted the church with unmatched zeal (thus Phil 3:5).

Why had Paul the Pharisee been so zealous in persecuting the church? It was not because Christians had in principle rejected the validity of the law. We know that the earliest Christians continued to observe even the regulations about circumcision and unclean foods. Nor was it simply because they believed that God's "anointed one" (in Hebrew, *Mashiah* ["Messiah"]; in Greek, *Christos* ["Christ"]), expected by many Jews, had already come in the person of Jesus. In fact, the Judaism of Paul's day tolerated various kinds of messianic sects and claims.

What was not generally tolerated, however, was belief in a Messiah who had *suffered* and who had been *crucified*. By and large, the Jewish expectation was that God's anointed would come as a king like David, a figure of heroic stature. True, Paul says nowhere that his hostility toward the church had been fueled by its belief in a crucified Messiah. We may infer that this was the case, however, from certain points that he comes later to emphasize about Jesus. One passage in particular deserves our careful reading.

Galatians 3:10–14

Here, as in most of Galatians, the apostle is writing about faith and righteousness. Against the position that he had held as a Pharisee, he now argues that righteousness is not established by obedience to the law. Rather, he says, righteousness comes only as a gift, received through faith. He supports this by appealing to several passages from the Jewish Scriptures. First, he interprets Deut 27:26 to mean that the law itself lays a curse upon those who rely upon it (v. 10). Next, he cites Hab 2:4 which links faith and righteousness ("The one who is righteous through faith will live"), and with that he contrasts Lev 18:5, which commends obedience of the law without saying a word about righteousness (vv. 11–12).

Finally, Paul makes use of a statement from Deut 21:22–23. It had been customary, after the execution of a criminal or an enemy, to display the corpse by hanging it on a tree (as in Josh 8:29, for example). However, the passage in Deuteronomy provides that the body is to be left there no more than one day. Otherwise, it would defile the whole land, since (according to the Greek version of Deut 21:23) "whoever is hung on wood has been cursed by God." This is the statement echoed by Paul in Gal 3:13: "Christ redeemed us from the curse of the law by becoming a curse for us – for it is written 'Cursed is everyone who hangs on wood.'"

The scriptural passages that Paul has introduced into his

discussion have involved him in some rather precarious reasoning. We see this especially in his use of the passages from Deuteronomy, and above all when he quotes the statement about a corpse hanging on wood. Why has Paul been drawn to this particular text? Could it not have been used *against* the church's faith that Jesus was the Messiah (in Greek: "Christ") of Jewish hopes?

The second question suggests an answer to the first. The statement of Deut 21:23 could have been, and probably was, quoted by Jews as a decisive objection to the church's proclamation of Jesus as Messiah. From their point of view, this crucified man of Nazareth could not have been the Messiah, since Scripture declares that a curse attaches to anyone who hangs on wood. It is likely that Paul himself, when a Pharisee, had employed the passage in this way, and that his concern to "destroy" the church had been prompted largely by its preaching of a crucified Messiah. This would help to explain why, once he has come to believe in Jesus as the Christ, he continues to refer to Deut 21:23. Now, as an apostle, he is concerned to show that the passage does not refute the gospel but supports it.

When Paul comments in another letter that the preaching of "Christ crucified" poses "a scandal [stumbling block] to Jews" (1 Cor 1:23), he knows whereof he speaks. That must have been exactly his own experience while he was still a devout Pharisee and a dedicated persecutor of the church.

Paul's Apostolic Call

What caused Paul to begin preaching the very gospel that he had formerly denounced as blasphemy? What changed this persecutor of the church into an apostle of its Lord? It is usual, in this connection, to speak of Paul's "conversion." The term is somewhat misleading, however, since it implies that he had

abandoned one religion in favor of another. That is definitely
not his own view of the matter. Rather, Paul came to believe
that the real children of Abraham are those who have received
the gospel and who live by faith in Christ (see, for example, Gal
3:6–9; Rom 2:28–29).

Therefore, in keeping with Paul's own emphasis, it is better
to speak of the decisive turning-point in his life as constituted
of a *revelation* and a *call*. Before examining the apostle's own
remarks on the subject, however, we must consider how his
radical turn-around is portrayed in Acts.

The Accounts in Acts

According to the narrative account in Acts 9:1–19, a blinding
light from heaven strikes Saul down as he journeys toward
Damascus in pursuit of Christians (vv. 1–3). Then he hears
Jesus' voice asking him, "Saul, Saul, why do you persecute
me?" (v. 4), and instructing him to proceed into Damascus
where he will receive further directions. Unable to see, he is
guided by his friends to the house of a certain Judas in "the
street called Straight" (vv. 8–9, 11). Meanwhile, a follower of
Jesus named Ananias has seen the Lord in a vision, and has
been directed to find Saul in the house of Judas (vv. 10–12).
Somewhat reluctantly, Ananias obeys the Lord's command
and, when he has located Saul, restores his sight (vv. 13–18a).
Thereupon Saul is baptized, eats, and regains his strength (vv.
18b–19).

This story, with a certain variation of details, is told twice
more in Acts, both times as a first-person account from Paul
himself (to the "Hebrews" of Jerusalem, 22:6–16; to King
Agrippa, 26:12–18). Common to all three accounts is the point
that Paul's missionary service is in response to a divine call
and commissioning. In chapter 9 we learn of this call only
indirectly, in the report of what the Lord told Ananias about

Paul's role (vv. 15–16). Then in chapter 22 we are told that Ananias had mediated the Lord's call to Paul (vv. 14–15). Finally, in chapter 26 it is said that the Lord himself issued the call immediately after addressing Paul on the road to Damascus (vv. 16–18). Despite these differences, and others, the essential content of the divine call remains the same: Paul has been chosen to preach Christ to the Gentiles as well as to the Jews (9:15), thus "to all the world" (22:15).

Paul's Own References

Paul's most important references to his apostolic call come in Gal 1:15–17 and 1 Cor 15:8–11. From an incidental remark that he *"returned* to Damascus" (Gal 1:17), it is apparent that he had been somewhere in that vicinity when he heard God's call (Gal 1:16). On this point, then, the accounts in Acts are confirmed. Paul himself, however, says nothing about a blinding light, any words spoken by Christ, anyone named Ananias, or his own baptism. The apostle's interest is almost exclusively in the source of his call and in its purpose.

Paul, no less than the author of Acts, attributes his call to God. It is significant that he thinks of this *only* as a "call," never as his own "decision" to become an apostle. Thus, like Israel's prophets, he is persuaded that he had been set apart for God's service even before he was born (Gal 1:15; note Isa 49:1 and Jer 1:5). Paul indicates that he had become aware of his calling when God favored him with a revelation of "his Son" (Gal 1:16). The rhetorical questions in 1 Cor 9:1 make the same point: "Am I not an apostle? Have I not seen Jesus our Lord?" He is convinced that, belated though it was, the Lord's appearing to him was like the appearances of the resurrected Christ to Peter and the other apostles (1 Cor 15:5–8). Paul acknowledges that, since he had been a persecutor of the church, he is "the least" among those who were apostles before him, "unfit to be called an apostle" (1 Cor 15:9; see also Gal 1:13–14). Yet for that very reason, he can point to *his* call as compelling evidence of God's unbounded grace (Gal 1:15; 1 Cor 15:10).

In Gal 1:16 Paul specifically says that God has called him to apostleship so that he can declare the gospel to the gentiles. The same purpose is presupposed, though not stated, in 1 Cor 15:8–11. It is particularly emphasized in Romans, where Paul describes himself as "an apostle to the Gentiles" (11:13), and as "a minister of Christ Jesus to the Gentiles in the priestly service of the gospel of God" (15:16). When he goes on to write of "what *Christ* has accomplished *through* [him] to win obedience from the Gentiles" (15:18), it is evident that he regards the success of his mission, no less than his apostleship itself, as God's doing.

The Apostle's New Perspective

Paul's transformation from devout Pharisee to devoted apostle of Christ involved fundamental changes in his thinking about Jesus' death, the law of Moses, and God's promises to Israel. Whether these changes contributed to Paul's conversion or resulted from it is a question that can be left open. It is more important to note what new direction his thinking took on each of these crucial matters.

First, after the Damascus experience Paul does not just concede but emphatically proclaims that the man from Nazareth who died on the cross is the Christ, God's anointed one. What the Pharisee had viewed as a "scandal" (1 Cor 1:23), the apostle now perceives as a saving event, the definitive instance of God's love. Paul can now affirm: "God proves his love for us in that while we still were sinners Christ died for us" (Rom 5:8). And further: "For Christ's love lays claim to us, since we have come to the judgment that 'one has died for all' ..."

(2 Cor 5:14, author's translation). Now too he can join with the church in declaring that Jesus was raised from the dead (for example, Rom 10:9), and that Jesus will come again at the close of this age (for example, 1 Thess 4:13–17; 1 Cor 11:26; 15:24–28).

Second, after Damascus Paul views the law of Moses in a very different way. Like every devout Jew, Paul the Pharisee had affirmed the law as "the embodiment of knowledge and truth," the one sure guide to God's will (note Rom 2:17–20). Thus, he had regarded obedience to the law's commandments as the way to righteousness, the way one stays "right" with God. It was this devotion to the law that had led him to reject as blasphemy the church's claims about Jesus. But Paul the apostle declares that the law itself bears witness to Jesus as the Christ. Instead of rejecting Jesus because of the law, he is now led by his faith in Christ to reject his previous understanding of the law. He no longer regards obedience to its statutes as the way to righteousness. Paul now maintains that one is "put right by [God's] grace as a gift, through the redemption that is in Christ Jesus" (Rom 3:24, author's translation).

Third, along with the apostle's new reading of the law goes a new understanding of God's promises to Israel. True, he remains convinced even after Damascus that the Jews are God's chosen people. He can still assert that "to them belong the adoption, the glory, the covenants, the giving of the law, the worship, and the promises; to them belong the patriarchs, and from them, according to the flesh, comes the Messiah" (Rom 9:4–5). Yet Paul no longer presumes that God's special relationship with the Jews excludes the Gentiles from God's promises, or allows them only second-class status within the people of God. He is now convinced that Israel's God is no less "the God of Gentiles" (Rom 3:29), and that God's people have been constituted "not from the Jews only but also from the Gentiles" (Rom 9:24). Now he boldly associates God's promise to Abraham with the gospel (Gal 3:6–18), and describes Abraham himself as "the ancestor of all who believe" (Rom 4:11). It makes no difference whether one is a Jew or a Gentile, circumcised or uncircumcised. Abraham's true descendants are those who live by faith.

Paul's Knowledge of Jesus

As we have observed, Paul came to believe that he had been set apart for apostleship even before his birth. Perhaps for this reason he writes as if his coming to faith and his call to apostleship were one and the same event. As he sees it, in response to a vision of the resurrected Jesus he had simultaneously accepted the gospel and committed himself to preach it to the Gentiles.

We can appreciate this as the testimony of a man of faith. But are we to believe that nothing in Paul's experience had prepared him for such a vision, or to respond as he did? Surely, what the church claimed about Jesus must have been known to him in some way, otherwise he would not have devoted himself to the church's destruction. There must have been talk about Jesus in the Pharisaic circles within which he moved. Had he also heard the church's claims about Jesus firsthand? At least in the process of persecuting the church, he would have observed how profoundly the gospel had touched the lives of many believers.

Some interpreters even suggest that Paul had heard the preaching of Jesus himself, or had at least seen Jesus before his crucifixion. The reasoning generally runs something like this: (1) Since Paul had studied in Jerusalem with a famous rabbi (Acts 22:3), it is possible that he witnessed the fateful events of the last week of Jesus' life. (2) Certain comments in Paul's letters suggest that he had been impressed with the way Jesus had conducted his ministry (for example, Rom 15:3, 2 Cor 10:1;

Phil 2:6–8). (3) Paul's remark in 2 Cor 5:16 seems to confirm that he did indeed have some firsthand knowledge of Jesus' earthly life. However, an examination of the passages cited as evidence shows that not one of these points is secure.

Acts 22:3

At the beginning of his speech to the Jews of Jerusalem, the Paul of Acts asserts that he had been "brought up in this city at the feet of Gamaliel, educated strictly according to our ancestral law ..." Gamaliel was a renowned Jerusalem rabbi of the mid-first century, and Paul certainly *could* have studied with him. But if he did, why hasn't he himself mentioned this in Phil 3:5–6? There, listing his Jewish "credentials," he says only that he was "circumcised on the eighth day, a member of the people of Israel, of the tribe of Benjamin, a Hebrew born of Hebrews; as to the law, a Pharisee; as to zeal, a persecutor of the church; as to righteousness under the law, blameless." That he does not write, "as to the law, a Pharisee *and a student of Gamaliel*" renders the statement attributed to Paul in Acts 22:3 very questionable. It is part of the "larger than life" portrait of Paul that we find in the Book of Acts.

Romans 15:3; 2 Corinthians 10:1; Philippians 2:6–8

These and similar passages suggest to some that Paul retained vivid, firsthand impressions of Jesus the man, which not even his vision of the resurrected Christ had entirely eclipsed. Thus (it is said), even as an apostle he remembered the "gentleness and kindness" of Jesus (2 Cor 10:1), that he had not tried to "please himself" (Rom 15:3), and that his ministry had been one of humble service to others (Phil 2:6–8). However, nothing in the contexts of these passages indicates that Paul's remarks stem from personal observations. On the contrary, in each of them we hear echoes of scriptural and other traditional formulations. Even more important, Paul's comments are not about Jesus' human characteristics and earthly ministry. Rather, they are affirmations about Jesus as Christ, Lord, and Son of God.

Both points are apparent in the case of Phil 2:6–8. These verses comprise the first stanza, and verses 9–11 the second stanza, of a hymn that Paul is quoting. There are echoes of the Jewish Bible in both stanzas – Isaiah 53 in the first, and Isaiah 45 in the second. Thus traditional concepts, not personal observations, have been employed in its composition. Moreover the subject of this hymn is not the earthly Jesus, but Jesus as the heavenly Christ (v. 6) and exalted Lord (vv. 9–11). It tells how Christ, declining to claim equality with God, demeaned himself among humankind (v. 7), became obedient even unto death (v. 8), and was then exalted by God to be Lord of the whole universe (vv. 9–11). This is the story of salvation, a story not limited to the space and time occupied by Jesus' earthly ministry. The humiliation and obedience mentioned in verse 8 are therefore references to the gracious self-abasement and self-sacrifice of the Son of God.

The same is true of Paul's comment that "Christ did not please himself" (Rom 15:3). This is an affirmation that Christ gave himself up unto death, not simply an observation about the way Jesus conducted his ministry. Were it the latter, some particular incident might have been related in order to back it up. As it is, Paul supports his point with a quotation from Psalm 69: "The insults of those who insult you have fallen on me" (v. 9). This psalm was one of several which the church of Paul's day read as scriptural testimonies to Christ's passion and death (see also v. 22, and compare Mark 15:36 and parallels).

Paul refers to "the gentleness and kindness of Christ" (2 Cor 10:1, author's translation) because he wants the Corinthians to know how he himself is trying to deal with them. It is doubtful, however, whether the reference is to Jesus' human traits. Elsewhere in this context Paul is thinking of Christ's status as Lord (see vv. 5, 7–8). Moreover, in Paul's Bible (the Greek version of the Jewish Scriptures) "kindness" is one of God's own characteristics (for example, Wisd 12:18 [NRSV: "mildness"]), and the messianic king is described as "gentle" (Zech 9:9, applied to Jesus in Matt 21:5). We may also note the spontaneous aside prompted by the thought of Christ's gentleness and kindness: "I who am humiliated when face to face with you, but bold to you when I am away!" (author's translation). This suggests that when he introduces the appeals in 2 Corinthians 10, as when he quotes the hymn in Philippians 2, Paul is thinking about the pre-existent Christ whose gentleness and kindness led to his profound humiliation.

2 Corinthians 5:16

In this part of 2 Corinthians, Paul is contending with people who have challenged his apostolic credentials. Specifically, he is concerned to show that ordinary measures of "success" do not apply when it comes to apostleship. It is in this connection that he comments (to translate the verse rather literally), "From now on, therefore, we know no one according to the flesh. Even though we once knew Christ according to the flesh, now we no longer know him that way." Sometimes this is interpreted as if the apostle were contrasting ordinary knowledge of the merely human ("fleshly") Jesus with "spiritual" knowledge of Jesus as the resurrected Christ. Should this be the case, Paul would be saying that as a Christian he knows Jesus to be *more* (or perhaps *other*) than a mere human being. One might then conclude that, sometime before his vision at Damascus, Paul had encountered the earthly Jesus.

The remark in 2 Cor 5:16 does not, however, support this conclusion. For one thing, the phrase "according to the flesh" does not connect with the name "Christ" (as if to refer to the *human* Jesus) but with the verb "know," describing how Christ is viewed. Moreover, here as elsewhere Paul uses the phrase to mean "according to worldly standards," or "from a worldly point of view." The apostle is saying (to translate more freely): "From now on we are evaluating no one with reference to worldly standards. Even though worldly standards once governed the way we understood Christ, that is no longer the case." The statement in itself does not contrast an "earthly Jesus" with a "heavenly" Christ. Nor does it help us to know whether Paul had ever seen or heard Jesus during his earthly ministry.

Summary

Paul never questions the historical reality of Jesus' life and ministry. There is no evidence, however, that Paul had ever seen or heard the earthly Jesus, let alone that he had ever met or conversed with him. What the apostle emphasizes is the vision that he had been granted of the resurrected Jesus, revealed as God's Son. Whatever Paul had known about Jesus before then, whether firsthand or secondhand, was of lesser importance to him. The vision was decisive.

Chapter 2

Paul's Knowledge about Jesus

The Information in Paul's Letters

Although Paul had never met or even seen the earthly Jesus, his surviving letters show that he had some knowledge *about* Jesus' ministry and message. To be sure, no letter includes anything like a summary of Jesus' earthly activities or teachings. But from the bits and pieces about Jesus' earthly life that do show up, it is possible to put together the following summary on Paul's behalf.

1. Jesus was born under the law (Gal 4:4), a Jew of David's line (Rom 1:3).
2. Jesus had more than one brother (1 Cor 9:5), one of whom was named James (Gal 1:19; 2:9, 12; 1 Cor 15:7).
3. Jesus had twelve special associates. One of them was Cephas (Gal 2:1–14, etc.), who was sometimes called "Peter" (Gal 2:7, 8); another was John (Gal 2:9).
4. Jesus taught that anyone who preached the gospel should be provided a living from the gospel (1 Cor 9:14). He also taught that neither partner in a marriage should seek a divorce (1 Cor 7:10–11).
5. One night, dining with his closest followers, Jesus spoke about his own death as something beneficial for them (1 Cor 11:23–25). Thereafter, he told them, they should break bread and drink wine in his memory. They were to regard the loaf as a token of his body and the cup as a token of "the new covenant" in his blood.
6. On that same night Jesus was betrayed (1 Cor 11:23).

19

7. Out of obedience to God's will (Phil 2:8), and in accordance with the Scriptures (1 Cor 15:3), Jesus willingly gave himself up to death for the sins of his followers (1 Cor 15:3; Gal 1:4).

8. Jesus' death was by execution on a cross (1 Cor 1:17–2:5; Gal 3:1, etc.), for which "the rulers of this age" were responsible (1 Cor 2:8; if 1 Thess 2:14–16 was written by Paul, which some scholars doubt, then he implicates "the Jews" as well).

9. The corpse of Jesus was placed in a tomb (1 Cor 15:4; Rom 6:4).

This is the only information about Jesus' teachings, life, and death that can be gleaned from Paul's letters. Did he know nothing about Jesus' virginal conception, or about his baptism by John? Did he know nothing about Jesus' mighty deeds, or about his association with sinners and tax collectors? Did he know nothing about Jesus' preaching of the kingdom of God, or about Jesus' interpretation of the law? Had he never heard the name of Jesus' betrayer? Was he uninformed about the circumstances of Jesus' arrest and trial?

In posing these questions – which are of course unanswerable – we must remember that even the earliest of the four Gospels was not written until after Paul's death. He could not have learned about Jesus by reading Matthew, Mark, Luke, or John. How, then, had he gained such knowledge as he did have about Jesus' earthly life? It is possible, though not certain, that written collections of Jesus' sayings, and perhaps of stories about Jesus, were already in existence during Paul's lifetime. But most of what he knew about Jesus he would probably have learned by word of mouth, from oral traditions. At first, certain of those traditions would have been known even beyond the circle of Jesus' own followers. They lived on, however, principally in the liturgies, the preaching, and the instructional activities of the church itself.

Jesus Traditions in the Early Church

Traditions about Jesus originated the very moment that the first person, whoever he or she may have been, began talking about Jesus to somebody else, whoever she or he may have been. Of course this would have happened during Jesus' own lifetime, and among those who had the closest contacts with him. But very soon other people must have started talking about Jesus, including folk who had never even seen him. They too, as they talked about him, were contributing to the formation of the Jesus traditions.

Anyone who talked about Jesus, including that anonymous first person who talked about him, would have done so both selectively and from a particular point of view. That was inevitable, since people tend to forget whatever holds little interest or importance for them and to remember and share what has been significant for them. Thus even in the process of talking about Jesus people were already *interpreting* him. While the facts about Jesus did not change, people would have perceived and reported those facts differently, and always in accord with their particular point of view. This means that the traditions known to Paul already would have been enriched with varied interpretations of Jesus' ministry and teaching.

Careful scholarly analysis has shown that Paul, like the authors of the Gospels, drew upon two kinds of oral traditions about Jesus. The subject of the earliest traditions, which started circulating almost as soon as Jesus began his ministry, is what he had said and done during his earthly life. We may call these the "pre-Easter traditions." Other traditions, which we may think of as "post-Easter," attest the significance that Jesus continued to have for his followers even after his death. It must be emphasized that in the earlier traditions, no less than in the later, there was no information about Jesus apart from interpretations of his significance.

Traditions about Jesus' Earthly Life

The traditions about Jesus' earthly life seem to have circulated mainly in the form of stories about him. This is not surprising, because stories are a more direct and vivid means of communication than concepts or generalizations. Some of the stories about Jesus concerned his relationship with John the baptizer, including accounts of his baptism by John (see Mark 1:2–11; Matt 11:2–19). Other stories were told about Jesus' relationship with his closest followers: about his calling them to be disciples (Mark 4:18–22), his instructing them (Mark 9:30–49), and his commissioning of them (Luke 10:1–12).

Perhaps surprisingly, there were also stories about Jesus' "keeping bad company" – about his friendly associations with those who were marginalized, or even treated with contempt by much of Jewish society. Among these were accounts of his reaching out to tax collectors and others of ill repute (see Luke 19:1–10; Matt 11:18–19), of his concern for persons usually regarded as unclean (Mark 1:40–45), and of his acceptance of women into his entourage (see Luke 8:1–3). Other stories described the healings and exorcisms that Jesus had performed (Mark 1:29–31; 5:1–20) and his feats of supernatural power (like multiplying loaves and fish, Mark 8:1–10, and stilling a raging storm, Mark 4:35–41). Jesus' confrontations with those who opposed him were likewise recounted (see, for example, Mark 2:1–3:6).

All of these pre-Easter narrative traditions were circulating in some form during Paul's lifetime, but there is only scant evidence of them in his surviving letters. There they show up just once, and then only at second hand when Paul is citing the eucharistic liturgy (1 Cor 11:23–25).

The stories about Jesus usually included references to things that he had said – for example, to those who had sought his help, asked him questions, or challenged his claims. But the church also remembered and handed down many sayings of Jesus that were not so closely tied to specific incidents in his ministry. This is true of the parables, and also of numerous proverbial, legal, prophetic, and apocalyptic sayings that were passed on in the tradition. There are indications that various collections of these separate sayings, perhaps topically organized, were circulating among the churches from a fairly early time. It was perhaps in such a collection, more or less loosely arranged, that Jesus' teachings were known to Paul (see, in particular, 1 Cor 7:10–11 and 9:14). Only later, in Matthew, Mark, and Luke, do we find them worked into overall narrative presentations of Jesus' ministry. One important example of this is the so-called "sermon on the mount" in Matthew 5–7. The gospel writer has presented this collection of sayings as if it were a single discourse which Jesus had delivered on one specific occasion.

Traditions about Jesus' Continuing Significance

In addition to certain pre-Easter traditions about the earthly Jesus, Paul drew on many post-Easter traditions about the crucified and risen Lord. These originated among Jesus' followers as they sought to express their confidence that Jesus continued to be present with them and significant for their lives. We find this conviction set forth in several kinds of narratives, and in the church's liturgies and creeds.

The most obvious examples of post-Easter *narratives* are the accounts of Jesus' passion and death (Mark 14–15), of an empty tomb (Mark 16:1–8), of Jesus' resurrection appearances (for example, Matthew 28), and of his ascension (Luke 24:50–51; Acts 1:6–9). But the stories told about Jesus' conception and birth should also be considered here (Matt 1:18–2:23; Luke 1:5–2:40), as well as the descriptions of Jesus' anticipated return at the Last Day (Acts 1:10–11; Mark 13:24–27). There are no traces of the narratives about Jesus' conception and birth, the empty tomb, or the ascension in Paul's letters (at least in the ones that have come down to us). What the apostle has drawn on especially – but very selectively – are accounts of Jesus' death (1 Cor 2:2; Gal 3:1) and reports about his resurrection appearances (see especially, 1 Cor 15:5–7). Traditional expressions of confidence that the Lord will return are also evident in his letters (1 Thess 4:16; 5:2).

The narrative traditions of the post-Easter church often underlie its *liturgical* traditions. Among the latter are hymns, prayers, benedictions, doxologies, and various eucharistic and baptismal formulas. It is from these liturgical traditions, not from the narrative traditions about Jesus' earthly ministry, that Paul has drawn the eucharistic words of "the Lord Jesus" which he cites in 1 Cor 11:23–25 (compare Mark 14:22–25 and parallels). Also, various baptismal formulations have been detected in his letters (for example, 1 Cor 12:12 and Gal 3:28), as well as benedictions, doxologies, and selections from the church's hymnody (for example, Phil 2:6–11). In various ways these liturgical traditions celebrate, acclaim, or invoke Jesus as the risen and living Lord, in whom the community of faith has its life and its hope.

The church's *creedal* traditions developed in response to a continuing need to define and defend its faith in Christ. Controversies among Christians of different viewpoints as well as challenges from non-Christians played a role in this development. The result, it must be emphasized, was not just one creed but varied, and sometimes divergent creedal formulations. A number of these are echoed in Paul's letters, of which Rom 1:3–4, 1 Cor 8:6, and 1 Cor 15:3–5 are particularly clear examples.

Paul's Access to the Traditions

How did Paul gain such familiarity with the church's traditions about Jesus? When, where, and from whom did he learn what Jesus had said and done? Under what circumstances was he introduced to the church's liturgies, creeds, and distinctive interpretations of Scripture? The available sources provide no ready answers to these questions.

According to Acts, following his Damascus vision Paul had spent "several days" in that city with Jesus' followers, including Ananias (9:17–19). There is no suggestion, however, that he was being instructed by those Damascus Christians. Rather, we are told that Paul "immediately . . . began to proclaim Jesus in the synagogues, saying, 'He is the Son of God'" (9:20). The Acts narrative has Paul next in Jerusalem, where Barnabas presents him to the twelve apostles. But here again, he is portrayed as a bold preacher of the gospel, not as one in need of instruction (9:26–28).

Our questions become yet more difficult to answer when we add to our considerations the evidence of Paul's own letters. He himself claims that, following his vision of Christ and call to apostleship, he conferred with no one. He mentions neither Ananias nor any other Damascus Christian. Moreover, Paul specifically emphasizes that he did *not* go to Jerusalem to meet the apostles. Instead, he says, he went off to Arabia (the independent Kingdom of Nabataea, to the east), and then returned to Damascus (Gal 1:16–17). Quite clearly, his concern as he writes to the Galatians is to underscore the divine origin both of his gospel and of his apostleship (see 1:1, 11–12).

This concern is still evident as Paul proceeds to describe his first contact, as a Christian, with those who were apostles before him:

Then after three years I did go up to Jerusalem to visit Cephas and stayed with him fifteen days; but I did not see any other apostle except

James the Lord's brother. In what I am writing to you, before God, I do not lie! (Gal 1:18–20)

Here Paul wishes to register three points: (a) he had been engaged in his apostolic work for several years prior to his first trip to Jerusalem; (b) he stayed in Jerusalem a relatively brief time; (c) he left the city without even having met most of the apostles. From this the Galatians are to conclude that Paul had needed nothing from the Jerusalem church by way of authorization or instruction in order to carry on his ministry.

Despite Paul's explicit disavowal, many interpreters believe that it must have been on this visit to Jerusalem mentioned in Gal 1:18–20 that Paul was introduced to the church's most cherished traditions about Jesus. In this connection one has to take account of the verb that is often translated "to visit" (NRSV, etc.). Although some have argued that the Greek verb can mean "to get information from," the linguistic basis for that interpretation is not secure. Moreover, such a meaning would go against Paul's concern to show that neither his gospel nor his apostleship derives from the Jerusalem apostles. Nevertheless, Paul does seem to draw a distinction between his *visit* with Peter and his merely *seeing* "James the Lord's brother" (v. 19). When we also take into account the fifteen-day duration of the visit, it becomes apparent that Paul did not just greet Peter in passing. He was probably in Jerusalem "to get acquainted with" him. This translation does justice both to the linguistic evidence and to the context.

Having established this, however, we are still left wondering what went on during that "get acquainted visit." What did Paul say to Peter? Did he tell him about his Pharisaic past, his vision at Damascus, and his activities in the three years since? More important for our present topic, what did Peter say to Paul? Did he inform him about Jesus' teachings, the events of his ministry, the circumstances of his death, and his resurrection appearances? That is not impossible; but to say more would be to enter into the realm of pure speculation.

Finally, there are these points to consider. However much Paul may have learned in Jerusalem, it is unlikely that he could have appropriated in those two weeks all of the traditions with which his letters show him to have been familiar. Moreover, and more importantly, many of the liturgical, creedal, and testimonial traditions with which Paul was in touch seem to have had their origin in Greek-speaking, Hellenistic Christianity. He is most likely to have encountered those traditions in Syrian Antioch, which was a prominent and early center of Hellenistic Christianity and later of Paul's ministry (Gal 2:11–14; see also Acts 11:22–26). But here again we are restricted by our sources, and can do little more than speculate.

Paul as a Bearer of Traditions

Paul's indebtedness to the church's traditions, including the traditions about Jesus, would be apparent even if he himself had never acknowledged it. A few examples of such traditions have already come to our attention, but there are many others. It is important to consider how the apostle has used each of them. First, however, we must ask whether this reliance on traditional materials can be reconciled with Paul's claim that his gospel came not from any human source, but was given by divine revelation.

Tradition and Revelation

In three notable passages in 1 Corinthians, Paul specifically acknowledges his dependence on the church's traditions. The first of these appears to be a reference to "the traditions" in general: "I commend you because you remember me in everything and maintain the traditions *just as I handed them on* to you" (1 Cor 11:2). Perhaps the core traditions of the faith are in mind here, like the creedal statement cited in 1 Cor 15:3–5. In any case, Paul does not hesitate to cast himself in the role of one who has "handed on" to others what he himself has received.

This is confirmed by a second passage in the same letter: "For *I received* from the Lord *what I also handed on* to you ... " (1 Cor 11:23–25). The tradition that Paul proceeds to quote is drawn from the church's eucharistic liturgy, into which a scene from the passion narrative had been incorporated: "that the Lord Jesus on the night when he was betrayed took a loaf of bread," etc. The apostle does not mean that he had received this directly "from the Lord" as a special revelation. The words "received" and "handed on" can only describe the sharing of a community's traditions. Divine oracles addressed to privileged individuals are described in other ways (see, for example, 2 Cor 12:8–9). Paul is suggesting only that the Lord's *authority* stands behind the words of the tradition that he cites.

The same technical terms for the transmission of tradition are present in yet a third passage, 1 Cor 15:3–5: "For *I handed on* to you as of first importance *what I in turn had received:* that 'Christ died for our sins ... and that he was raised on the third day ... and that he appeared ... '" Where exactly Paul's quotation ends is not quite clear. It is entirely clear, however, that he attributes this affirmation to the church's tradition.

In themselves, these three passages seem straightforward enough. Without hesitation or qualification the apostle refers to his having been a bearer of important Christian traditions. But this leaves us unprepared for what we find him claiming in Gal 1:11–12:

[11]The gospel that was preached by me is not of human origin; for I did not receive it from a human source, nor was I taught it; [12]rather, (it

was entrusted to me) through a revealing of Jesus Christ. (Author's translation.)

The words in parentheses have been supplied for the sake of the translation, since Paul himself leaves one verb unexpressed. The gap has been filled in by borrowing a term that the apostle uses a few paragraphs later when referring to his gospel (see Gal 2:7). The NRSV rendering, "I received it," is misleading, because Paul is drawing a sharp distinction between what he has *received* from other people and what has been *revealed* to him by God. The revelation that he is thinking of here is doubtless the one granted to him at Damascus, from which both his apostleship and his gospel derive (see Gal 1:1, 15–16).

But this leaves us with a question. How can the apostle claim for his gospel the immediacy of divine revelation (Gal 1:11–12) and still acknowledge his role in handing on ecclesiastical traditions (1 Cor 11:2, 23; 15:3)? An answer is available once we have noticed that Paul distinguishes the gospel as such from statements about the gospel. *The gospel itself* he associates above all with God's working in Christ for salvation. It was this gospel that he had been granted by divine revelation and that has become for him a life-transforming event. He had not received it from any human source, not even from the earliest apostles. What he had received from other believers were *statements about* God's saving work in Christ. No matter how well these may describe or explain the gospel, they do not in themselves constitute the saving event.

This distinction may be illustrated and confirmed by looking carefully at 1 Cor 15:1–3. In verses 1–2 Paul writes of having "proclaimed" (literally: "gospelled") his gospel in Corinth. He does not say that he had "handed it on," because he does not regard it as part of the tradition that he had received from others. To be sure, he reminds the Corinthians that they had "received" the gospel. In this context, however, the point is not that it had come to them as a tradition, but that they had *accepted* it. Thus it has become for them a saving event, in which they continue to "stand" (v. 1) and through which they are "being saved" (v. 2). But in verse 3 Paul's terminology changes. Here a creedal statement about Christ's death and resurrection is indeed introduced as one of the church's traditions: he had "handed on" to the Corinthians what he had himself "received." Although the apostle does not disparage such traditions, he does not understand his ministry to be defined and empowered by them, but only by the gospel itself.

Tradition and Interpretation

In our everyday speech the word "traditional" is commonly used to describe things we view as unchanged and unchanging. We often speak, for example, of traditional clothes, or of traditional behavior, or of traditional ideas. In fact, however, traditions are never static. Because traditions are, by definition, *handed down* (whether in a family, an ethnic group, a nation, or some other kind of community), they are always in motion. They are constantly undergoing interpretation. This process is sometimes automatic, sometimes deliberate; sometimes more evident, sometimes less so. But traditions inevitably change, and if they do not, they die. They do not constitute a stagnant pool, but a running brook.

This was certainly true of the traditions about Jesus which Paul, having himself received, then handed on to his churches. They *lived* precisely as they were adapted, interpreted, and applied. The apostle himself, as a bearer of those traditions, was at the same time an interpreter of them. His use of the traditions about Jesus' teaching deserves special consideration, and is taken up in chapter 3. First, however, we need to consider examples of how Paul drew on the liturgical and creedal traditions about Jesus, and described him with various traditional titles and images.

Paul's Use of Liturgical and Creedal Traditions

1 Corinthians 11:17–34

In verses 17–22 Paul is sharply critical of what happens when his Corinthian congregation assembles for the Lord's supper. He does not doubt the accuracy of reports that on these occasions there is divisiveness, drunkenness, and general disorder. It is in this connection that the apostle quotes some lines from the eucharistic liturgy (vv. 23b–25):

23bThe Lord Jesus on the night when he was betrayed took a loaf of bread, 24and when he had given thanks, he broke it and said, "This is my body that is for you. Do this in remembrance of me." 25In the same way he took the cup also, after supper, saying, "This cup is the new covenant in my blood. Do this, as often as you drink it, in remembrance of me."

We have already noted how Paul introduces this citation, identifying the words as traditional: "For I received from the Lord what I also handed on to you ... " (v. 23a). It is therefore clear that the apostle is not conveying this tradition to his congregation for the first time. He is reminding them of words which are part of the liturgy that they use every time they assemble to celebrate the eucharist.

But Paul does more than just recite the traditional words. To those words he adds his own: "For as often as you eat this bread and drink the cup, you proclaim the Lord's death until he comes" (v. 26). This statement is not part of the liturgy (nothing like it stands in the eucharistic passages in the Synoptic Gospels: Matt 26:26–29; Mark 14:22–25; Luke 22:15–20). Rather, it is the apostle's *interpretive comment* on the traditional words, and therefore on the meaning of the eucharist itself. The Corinthians need to remember that they gather as a community of persons for whom Christ died, and for whom Christ will come again. If, however, they continue to bestow privilege upon those who are better off and to humiliate those of lesser means, then it is not truly the Lord's supper of which they partake.

The traditional words of the liturgy, along with Paul's interpretive comment on those, provide the basis for the exhortations and warnings which conclude the passage (vv. 27–29, 33–34a):

[27]Whoever, therefore, eats the bread or drinks the cup of the Lord in an unworthy manner will be answerable for the body and blood of the Lord. [28]Examine yourselves, and only then eat of the bread and drink of the cup. [29]For all who eat and drink without discerning the body, eat and drink judgment against themselves.

[33]So then, my brothers and sisters, when you come together to eat, wait for one another. [34a]If you are hungry, eat at home, so that when you come together, it will not be for your condemnation.

One should not miss the point of Paul's comments on eating and drinking Christ's body and blood "in an unworthy manner," and "without discerning the body." It is of course the body of Christ to which he refers, but not only as that is represented in the bread and wine on the eucharistic table. More especially, Paul views the assembled community itself as Christ's body. Thus, he is warning the Corinthians that by dishonoring *one another* they are in fact dishonoring the body of Christ, of which they are all members by reason of his saving death. It is to help him make this point that he has cited the traditional eucharistic words of Jesus.

Philippians 1:27–2:18

Here Paul is appealing to the members of his Philippian congregation to conduct themselves as befits their status as a Christian community. About midway in these appeals, in 2:6–11, he seems to be quoting one of the church's hymns.

Although he does not specifically identify it as drawn from the hymnic tradition, the passage has an unmistakable rhythmic structure and falls easily into two distinct stanzas. Like most early Christian hymns, its subject is the heavenly Christ (see above, p. 16).

The first stanza (vv. 6–8) portrays Christ's divesting himself of any claim to divine status and becoming "obedient to the point of death." In consequence of this, according to the second stanza (vv. 9–11), God has established him as the "Lord," before whom every creature in the whole universe bows low in adoration and praise. Proposals abound about the origins of this hymn, and about the particular liturgical settings in which it may have been used. Neither of these questions, however, can be answered with any confidence.

Although both the source and the original liturgical setting of the hymn remain obscure, it is not difficult to see why and how Paul has quoted it in this letter. Because the Christians of Philippi are at risk from certain (unnamed) opponents (1:28), the apostle urges them to stand firm, "striving side by side with one mind for the faith of the gospel" (1:27). This call for courage and unity in the midst of adversity is continued in 2:2b–4:

2bBe of the same mind, having the same love, being in full accord and of one mind. Do nothing from selfish ambition or conceit, but in humility regard others as better than yourselves. 4Let each of you look not to your own interests, but to the interests of others.

It is at this point that Paul quotes the hymn, introducing it with an appeal to "be so minded among yourselves as is also appropriate in Christ Jesus ... " (v. 5; author's translation).

Clearly, the hymn is quoted in order to support the call to "live ... in a manner worthy of the gospel of Christ" (1:27). This is confirmed when, following the quotation, a further appeal (2:12–13) is introduced by the word "therefore":

[12]Therefore, my beloved, just as you have always obeyed me, not only in my presence, but much more now in my absence, work out your own salvation with fear and trembling; [13]for it is God who is at work among you, enabling you both to will and to work for his good pleasure. (NRSV, modified.)

Why has Paul chosen to invoke this *particular* hymn in support of his appeals? Above all, probably, because it rehearses the "story of salvation" by which his readers have been constituted, in Christ, as a community of faith. It thus supports the appeal that they conduct themselves in ways that are appropriate to their life in Christ (see 1:27; 2:5). In addition, the hymn draws special attention to Christ's humbling himself and becoming obedient to God's will. Thereby it also reinforces the apostle's specific calls for humility (2:3–4) and obedience (2:12). We should observe, however, that it is not the moral character of the earthly Jesus that is praised in the hymn. Rather, it praises Jesus himself, as Savior and Lord. And it is Christ as Lord who is probably uppermost in Paul's mind, as well, when he quotes the hymn to support his appeals. In Christ the Philippians have been given more than just a moral example. In him they have been granted new life.

Many interpreters believe that in the process of quoting this hymn, Paul has left his own theological fingerprints on it. In the hymn itself, the first stanza perhaps concluded with the words, "obedient to the point of death" (v. 8). If so, the specification of the manner of Jesus' death, "even death on a cross," would be Paul's interpretive addition. This remains a theory, but it is altogether plausible. As we shall see, it is characteristically Pauline to emphasize that Jesus was put to death on a cross.

2 Corinthians 5:11–15

In this passage the apostle is making use of a traditional creedal statement about Christ, although he quotes and interprets it in his own way. The formulation as Paul knew it from the tradition is probably the one we find in 1 Cor 15:3, "Christ died for us" (Rom 5:8; 1 Thess 5:10). In the present passage, there is a further variation of the formula (vv. 14–15):

[14]For the love of Christ lays claim to us, since we have come to the conviction that *one has died for all*; therefore all have died. [15]And *he died for all*, so that those who live might live no longer for themselves, but for him *who died and was raised for them*. (NRSV, modified)

The traditional creedal statement about Christ's death is echoed at three points in these lines: in the affirmations that "one has died for all" and that "he has died for all," and in the description of Christ as the one "who died and was raised for them."

The tradition is invoked, first, to support the statement that Christ's love "lays claim to us." Implicitly, this is an appeal to live in accordance with the love manifested in Christ. Since the apostle regards Christ's death as the defining instance of God's love (see especially, Rom 5:8; 8:31–39), it is not surprising that he should allude to the creedal affirmation about that in order to underscore his point. That statement, in turn, supports a second (implicit) appeal, that those for whom Christ has died ought to "live no longer for themselves, but for him."

When citing this particular creedal tradition, Paul makes two extremely important interpretive moves. First, he alters the traditional, "Christ has died for our sins" (or "for us"), to "*One* has died for *all*." The emphasis falls on the word "all," by which Paul means not just "all who believe," but the whole of humankind. Here, as in subsequent references to the "new creation" in Christ (5:17) and the reconciliation of "the world" (5:19), he envisions the universal scope of Christ's saving work.

Paul's other interpretive move, more explicit, comes in his remark about the consequence of Christ's death. The creedal statement as he knew it in the tradition may well have presumed a "substitutionary" interpretation of Christ's death. According to this view Christ died *in our place*, having taken it upon himself to pay the due penalty "for our sins." Paul, however, interprets the creedal statement about Christ's death in a strikingly different way. He does not say, "One has died for all; *therefore all may live.*" Instead, his conclusion is that "*all have died.*" That is, by reason of Christ's death all have "died" to the old age; for in Christ everything old has passed away, and there is "a new creation" (5:17). Those who affirm and commit themselves to this new creation ("those who live," v. 15) are to live "no longer for themselves," but for Christ – just as he has died, and continues to live, for them.

Paul's Use of Traditional Titles and Images for Jesus

It is often difficult for us to find words to express how some particular person has touched and perhaps transformed our lives. That was exactly the experience of the earliest Christians, as they sought to put into words the significance that Jesus had for them. Along with his name, "Jesus," and sometimes even in place of this name, they employed various titles and images to help express, however partially, their experience and understanding of him.

Traditional Titles

Several of the traditional titles for Jesus have found their way into Paul's letters. Primarily, the apostle refers to Jesus as "Christ" (more than 250 times, alone or in combination) and "Lord" (more than 150 times, alone or in combination). There are, however, only a few specific references to Jesus as God's Son (only 15 times), and the title "Savior" appears but once (Phil 3:20) in the letters that are certainly Paul's own. Occasionally, to be sure, Paul simply uses the name, "Jesus" (17 times), but that is not to call attention to Jesus' earthly life as such. In some instances, for example, it is to stress that Jesus is "Lord" (Rom 10:9; 1 Cor 12:3; Phil 2:10); in others, Jesus' death and resurrection are particularly in view (Rom 8:11; 2 Cor 4:10–14).

"Christ" derives from the Greek word *Christos* which, like the Hebrew word *Mashiah* ("Messiah"), means "anointed one." In ancient Israel, persons perceived to have been specially commissioned for significant tasks, including prophets and kings, were regularly described as "anointed" by God. This usage was continued in the Judaism of Jesus' time, when certain Jews looked forward to the coming of a political (or priestly) "anointed one" (Messiah). Those who believed that Jesus was the fulfillment of Israel's hopes naturally found it meaningful to think of him as God's Messiah. It is clearly Jesus to whom Paul has reference when he includes "the Messiah" in a list of blessings God has granted to the Jews (Rom 9:4–5):

[4]They are Israelites, and to them belong the adoption, the glory, the covenants, the giving of the law, the worship, and the promises; [5]to them belong the patriarchs, and from them, according to the flesh, comes the Messiah, who is over all, God blessed forever. Amen.

This, however, is the only certain place where Paul actually employs "Christ" as a title, to mean "*the* Christ," the Messiah. Elsewhere he uses "Christ" as simply one of Jesus' names, with no apparent intention to describe Jesus specifically as the "anointed one."

While there are also places where "Lord" is little more than part of Jesus' name, its titular function is never entirely lost. In both Aramaic (the language of the earliest, Palestinian Christians) and Greek, "lord" was often a title of simple respect, like "sir" in English. It could also be used, however, of someone – like a king, or even God – who exercised special power and authority. This is its meaning when applied to Jesus, both in the traditions to which Paul was heir and by the apostle himself. Thus, the acclamation of Jesus as "Lord" in the hymn of Phil 2:6–11 (v. 10) is an affirmation of his exalted, sovereign status. Paul himself regularly employs the title when he wishes to emphasize or appeal to Jesus' authority and power (for example, 1 Cor 5:4; 6:14; 7:10, 25; 9:14; 14:37; 2 Cor 10:8, 18; 13:10).

In almost half of his fifteen references to Jesus as God's "Son," Paul is echoing some kind of a traditional formulation. The title seems to have been used particularly in statements about Jesus' incarnation and death (see Rom 8:3, 32; Gal 2:20; 4:4). When Paul applies the title in his own way, his concern is ordinarily to suggest the closeness of Jesus' relationship to God (for example, in Rom 5:10; Gal 1:16). However, the apostle's use of the title is also a reminder that, according to his understanding, Jesus himself will be subjected, finally, to the Father (see 1 Cor 15:28).

The one instance of the title, "Savior," tells us little about Paul's view of Jesus: "Our citizenship is in heaven, and it is from there that we are expecting a Savior, the Lord Jesus Christ" (Phil 3:20). Just possibly, Paul has adapted this statement, along with the one following ("He will transform the body of our humiliation that it may be conformed to the body of his glory, by the power that also enables him to make all things subject to himself," v. 21), from a familiar creed. Be that as it may, "Savior" indicates only in a general way that Christ at his expected return will bring the work of salvation to its appropriate conclusion. (Compare 1 Thess 1:10, almost certainly a traditional formulation of this hope.)

Traditional Images

Some of the images that Paul applies to Jesus are traditional; others are probably original with him. Among the traditional images, probably, we should count the description of Jesus as a passover Lamb (1 Cor 5:7), and the more frequent instances where he is described or portrayed as judge (for example, Rom 2:16; 1 Cor 4:4–5). Numerous other images for Jesus are traditional in that they have been derived from Scripture, either by the church before Paul or by the apostle himself. Thus, combining Isa 8:14 and 28:16, Jesus is presented as a "stumbling stone" (Rom 9:32–33). Again, he is identified as "the spiritual rock" (1 Cor 10:4) by which God had provided Israel with water in the wilderness (Exod 17:6; Num 20:7–11). And in other places he is portrayed as a second Adam, through whom righteousness and life have overcome the sin and death brought into the world by the first Adam (Rom 5:12–21; 1 Cor 15:20–22, 45–49). To these we may add Paul's identification of Jesus with the "root of Jesse" (Rom 15:12, citing Isa 11:10). Certain other descriptions of Jesus (for example, "a life-giving spirit," 1 Cor 15:45; the "Yes" of God's promises, 2 Cor 1:19–20) perhaps originated with Paul himself.

Conclusion

Paul shares the belief of the earliest Christians that Jesus is the Messiah (Greek, *Christos*), God's anointed one. But except for Rom 9:5, he uses the traditional title, "Christ," only as one of Jesus' names, not to call attention to Jesus as the Messiah. It is a different matter with the titles "Lord" and "Son of God," however. These he certainly does employ as titles for Jesus, partly as they had been used in the tradition, and partly in his own way.

The images Paul applies to Jesus – those he draws from the tradition as well as his own – are often more expressive of his assessment of Jesus than the christological titles. Yet neither the images nor the titles, nor all of these taken together, are sufficient indicators of the apostle's thinking about Jesus. We can determine this only by considering the whole of what Paul says about his gospel.

Chapter 3

Sayings of Jesus in Paul's Letters

Introduction

Although he did not know the historical Jesus, there is no doubt that Paul was acquainted with at least some of the teachings attributed to him. Whether he knew those as oral traditions, or perhaps in the form of a written collection of sayings, we do not know. In either case, they were among those valued traditions of the church to which Paul was a grateful heir.

It is striking, however, how little use the apostle actually makes of Jesus' teachings. For example, he invokes none of the parables which later on were given such prominence in the Synoptic Gospels. Moreover, he has very little to say about the Reign of God, even though that is a fundamental theme in both the sayings and parable traditions. True, not all of Paul's letters have survived, and we have no transcripts of his actual preaching. Yet the sources we do have probably give us an accurate picture. As we shall see (chapter 4), Paul focuses his attention neither on the teachings of Jesus nor on Jesus' Palestinian ministry. His attention is focused, rather, on Jesus the crucified Messiah and the risen Lord.

It is important, nonetheless, to take account of the places and ways in which Paul does make use of the sayings tradition. As it happens, there are only three certain points in his letters – 1 Cor 7:10, 9:14, and 11:23–25 – where "the Lord" (meaning Jesus) is specifically identified as the source of words which are also attributed to Jesus in the Synoptic Gospels. We have already examined the eucharistic words in 1 Cor 11:23–25 (chapter 2), since those were probably known to Paul from the liturgy, not from the sayings tradition as such. It remains for us now to consider the other two instances, as well as several special cases (1 Cor 14:37: 2 Cor 12:8–9; 1 Thess 4:15–17). We must also consider the possibility that Paul has sometimes drawn on the sayings tradition without actually citing Jesus as his authority.

1 Corinthians 7:10–11

The Context

Beginning in 1 Corinthians 7 Paul is addressing a series of topics which have been raised in a letter that he has received from his Corinthian congregation (see 7:1a). The various specific issues discussed in chapter 7 all derive from the basic question whether it is appropriate for Christians to engage in sexual intercourse. Some of Paul's Corinthian converts seem to have believed that such relationships were incompatible with their baptism into Christ. Accordingly, some single Christians were deciding not to marry and some married Christians were divorcing their spouses. Other Corinthian Christians, it appears, were practicing celibacy within marriage. This is the situation which has called forth the directives and appeals of chapter 7.

Among the basic points that Paul wants to establish are the following:

(1) Sexual intercourse is not incompatible with one's new life in Christ, provided that it takes place between a husband and wife who remain faithful to one another (see, for example, 7:2, 28, 36).

(2) Still, since only a short time remains before the Lord's return (7:29–31) it is better to be single, as Paul himself is

(7:7–8). Single persons, he believes, are less encumbered with worldly cares and better able to devote themselves totally to the Lord (7:32–35).

(3) Celibacy, however, is a gift, and it has not been granted to all (7:7). For this reason, unmarried believers who do not have the gift of celibacy should commit themselves to a marriage relationship (7:9, 36).

(4) There should be no long-term abstention from sexual intercourse within a marriage (7:3–6). While for those who are single only celibacy is appropriate, for those who are married celibacy is never appropriate.

(5) When both partners to a marriage are Christians, there should be no divorce (7:10–11). Even where one partner is not a Christian, the marriage should continue for as long as it is harmonious (7:12–16).

The Lord's Instruction

It is in connection with the issue of divorce that Paul appeals to a saying of Jesus (1 Cor 7:10–11):

[10]To the married I give instruction – not I but the Lord – that the wife should not separate from her husband [11](but if she does separate, let her remain unmarried or else be reconciled to her husband), and that the husband should not divorce his wife. (NRSV, modified)

It is significant that Paul interrupts himself to make it clear that it is not he but the Lord who is "giving instruction" in this matter. It is also significant that he has not employed the name "Jesus," but one of the church's titles for Jesus. Neither here nor elsewhere does the apostle refer to Jesus as a "teacher," or use a phrase like "the teaching of Jesus." As we know from the Gospels, divorce was one of the topics on which Jesus offered instruction during the course of his ministry. But here it is Jesus "the Lord" not Jesus the teacher whose authority is invoked.

Paul himself seems to be responsible for the remark which most translators, correctly, place in a parenthesis. That remark does not belong to the saying proper but addresses a particular circumstance not encompassed in the saying: What if a divorce occurs anyway? In itself, then, the Lord's instruction as Paul knew it would have been: "The wife should not separate from her husband and the husband should not divorce his wife." The verbs "to separate" and "to divorce" are used interchangeably here. Thus, as Paul cites it the saying is an unqualified prohibition of divorce.

The Pre-Synoptic Tradition

Like Paul, the authors of the Synoptic Gospels were acquainted with a saying of Jesus about divorce. In all, there are four passages where this tradition is evident: Matt 5:31–32, Matt 19:3–9, Mark 10:2–12, and Luke 16:18.

In Luke, Jesus' saying about divorce is one of many that he offers to his disciples during the course of a long journey toward Jerusalem (9:51–19:27). The divorce saying, however, has no clear connection with those which precede and follow it. In Matthew 5 the saying is one of several statements in the Sermon on the Mount in which a word of Jesus has been set over against a provision of the law ("You have heard it said ... but I say").

In both Matthew 19 and Mark the divorce saying has a narrative setting. In each case Jesus' comments are offered in response to a hostile question with which he has been challenged by some Pharisees. According to Mark's version of the encounter Jesus is asked whether divorce is ever permissible (10:2). In effect, he is being challenged to take a stand either for or against the law of Moses, according to which a husband was permitted to divorce his wife (Deut 24:1–2). The question is different in Matthew. Assuming that Jesus does indeed accept what the law says about divorce, the Pharisees ask him to declare himself on a much-discussed matter of interpretation: On what grounds may a man divorce his wife? May he do so for any reason whatever, or only for some particular reason(s) (19:3)?

Turning to the sayings themselves, it is evident that a distinction must be made between the Marcan and Lucan versions on the one hand, and the Matthean version on the other. According to both Mark and Luke, Jesus' prohibition of divorce had been absolute:

Mark 10—[11]He said to them, "Whoever divorces his wife and marries another commits adultery against her; [12]and if she divorces her husband and marries another, she commits adultery."

Luke 16—[18]Anyone who divorces his wife and marries another commits adultery, and whoever marries a woman divorced from her husband commits adultery.

In the Marcan narrative this absolute prohibition of divorce is supported with citations from Gen 1:27 (God created male and female) and 2:24 (a man and a woman "become one flesh"). It is also backed up by the admonition, "What God has joined together, let no one separate" (10:9).

These same citations and the same admonition are present in Matthew 19 (vv. 4–6). Here, however, the law's allowance for divorce is accepted, with the explanation that it is a concession to human weakness (v. 7). Thus an "exception clause" appears in the Matthean version, in both of its occurrences:

Matthew 5—[32]But I say to you, that anyone who divorces his wife, *except on the ground of unchastity*, causes her to commit adultery; and who ever marries a divorced woman commits adultery.

Matthew 19—[9]And I say to you, whoever divorces his wife *except for unchastity*, and marries another commits adultery.

The version of the saying Paul knew must have been similar to the one which was later taken up into the Gospels of Mark and Luke. Paul, too, understands Jesus' prohibition of divorce to have been absolute. Moreover, the versions known to Paul and to Mark take account of Roman law, according to which wives as well as husbands had the right to initiate a divorce. That was not the case in Jewish law, nor is it envisioned in either Matthew or Luke. For two reasons, then, many scholars have concluded that the earliest surviving form of the saying is the one found in Luke: (1) it reflects the Palestinian–Jewish setting of Jesus' ministry (it presupposes that only a husband has the legal right to initiate a divorce); (2) it is more likely that a strict prohibition was subsequently eased than that a provision for exceptions was later deleted.

1 Corinthians 7:12–16

Immediately following his citation of the Lord's prohibition of all divorces (vv. 10–11), Paul continues (vv. 12–13):

[12]To the rest I say – I and not the Lord – that if any believer has a wife who is an unbeliever, and she consents to live with him, he should not divorce her. [13]And if any woman has a husband who is an unbeliever, and he consents to live with her, she should not divorce him.

There must have been numerous instances known to Paul where a husband or wife had accepted the gospel while the spouse had not. In that case, should the Christian partner remain in the marriage? Since belonging to Christ precludes union with a prostitute, as Paul himself has insisted (1 Cor 6:12–20), might it not also preclude remaining with a pagan spouse? The apostle says no, the Christian is not to seek divorce from an unbelieving partner. Thus far Paul is in full accord with the saying of Jesus that he has just cited.

Why, then, does the apostle emphasize that this is strictly his own counsel, *not* the Lord's? Many interpreters take this to mean that he doesn't know of any saying of Jesus that deals with the special case of a "mixed marriage." This possibility is suggested by the way Paul introduces a later topic: "Now concerning virgins, I have no rule from the Lord, but I give my opinion as one who by the Lord's mercy is trustworthy" (7:25; NRSV, modified). We may suppose that the apostle would *like* to have some instruction from Jesus about virgins. But since he hasn't any, he proceeds to offer his own judgment, having carefully identified it as such. Perhaps, then, verse 12 should be interpreted accordingly: "To anyone whose wife remains an unbeliever I say – since there is no instruction about this from the Lord, I am offering my own opinion – that if she consents to live with him ..."

The apostle's wording, however, allows of another interpretation. In distinction from the way he introduces his later counsel to virgins (v. 25), Paul does not say, in verse 12, that he *has* no instruction from the Lord. He only indicates that the directives about mixed marriages are his own, *not* the Lord's. Thus the apostle could mean that on this subject he is *departing* from the Lord's instruction. In fact, he does exactly that in verse 15. There he counsels that in one particular circumstance divorce is permissible: "If [in the case of a believer married to an unbeliever] the unbelieving partner separates, let it be so; *in such a case the brother or sister is not bound.* It is to peace that God has called you" (my italics). Clearly, from Paul's own point of view it is better to let a contentious marriage be dissolved than to abandon one's faith in order to please an unbelieving spouse.

1 Corinthians 9:14

The Context

Following the counsels about sex, marriage, and divorce in 1 Corinthians 7, Paul takes up the question of meat that has been left over from pagan sacrificial rites (8:1–11:1). At issue is whether it is even permissible for Christians to eat such meat, which was regularly sold in the public market or which might be offered at dinner by a non-Christian host. Some members of the Corinthian congregation were abstaining from it, perhaps thinking that it would be blasphemous to partake, or that they might be seduced back into paganism. Others saw no harm in eating the meat, arguing that the gods of the pagans don't really exist anyway (chapter 8).

In principle Paul agrees that Christians have the "right" (8:9; NRSV: "liberty," 8:9) to eat meat that comes from pagan temples (for example, 10:27). In practice, however, he counsels restraint for the sake of those who believe otherwise, their conscience "being weak" (that is, unenlightened; see 8:7–12 and 10:28–29). In this connection the apostle commends his own personal decision. He has resolved not to exercise his right to eat such meat if that would cause a Christian brother or sister to lapse back into unbelief (8:13).

The discussion in 1 Corinthians 9 follows from and continues Paul's commendation of his own conduct. While the question about eating meat from pagan temples is still the underlying subject, that is not specifically mentioned again until chapter 10. Here in chapter 9 Paul offers an example of another decision to give up one of his rights. Although his living expenses, like those of every apostle, are to be cared for by the churches (9:4–5), he has not claimed them from the Corinthians, nor will he (9:15–18). As in the case of meat from pagan temples, he is determined to give up whatever might hinder obedience to the gospel.

For the Corinthians (or at least many of them) Paul's failure to accept support from their congregation has raised a serious question. Is it perhaps because he does not really have full apostolic authority that he declines to exercise an apostle's right? For this reason, 1 Corinthians 9 is in part a defense of Paul's apostolic status (see v. 3) and an explanation of why he has not claimed what all apostles are due. However, it is in support of his *right* to expenses, not to defend his refusal of them, that Paul quotes a saying of Jesus.

The Lord's Decree

In the course of the discussion in 1 Corinthians 9, Paul offers five reasons why he is entitled to have his living expenses paid for by the Corinthians. These are, in order:

(1) All "other apostles," as well as "the brothers of the Lord and Cephas" receive such support (9:5). Implicitly, this is an appeal to what is equitable. Every other apostle, as well as Jesus' brothers and Peter, have received expenses. Paul and Barnabas have exactly that same right (9:6; see also, v. 12a).

(2) Other kinds of laborers are supported from the work in which they are primarily engaged (9:7). Thus soldiers are paid by the state they serve, those who plant vineyards eat of their fruit, and shepherds receive the milk of the flocks that they tend. None of these are dependent on a secondary occupation for their livelihood. Similarly, Paul has a right to expect that his needs will be cared for by those to whom he ministers. He should not have to work for a living at the same time that he is laboring as an apostle. (9:6).

(3) It is specified in the law of Moses that farmers are entitled to live off of the crops that they have grown and harvested (9:8–12a). The apostle's proof-text for this is Deut 25:4 (quoted in v. 9), where it is stipulated that an ox should be allowed to eat of the grain that it has been harnessed to thresh. Paul does not take the text at its word, however, but interprets it to mean that a farmer has a right to the produce of his field (v. 10). With this, the Corinthians should be able to see how the text applies to Paul's rights, for he has sown the gospel among them (v. 11; compare 1 Cor 3:5–9 – Paul is a planter, and the Corinthians are "God's field").

(4) Those who serve in temples get their food from the

temple (9:13). The reference here is probably to the temple in Jerusalem and Jewish practice (see Num 18:8–32; Deut 18:1–5), although the same could have been said about the practice in pagan temples.

(5) Finally, and perhaps as the crowning touch, Paul appeals to what "the Lord decreed" (author's translation). His direction, as the apostle reports it, was "that those who proclaim the gospel should get their living by the gospel" (9:14). The saying behind Paul's reference is evidently one which was later taken up as well into Matthew and Luke. That saying, according to the Matthean version is: "laborers deserve their food" (Matt 10:10b). The Lucan version, perhaps the earlier, reads: "the laborer deserves to be paid" (Luke 10:7). In this saying the word "laborer(s)" – which can also be translated as "worker(s)" – refers to those whom Jesus sent out to preach his message concerning the Reign of God.

Paul's Use of the Saying

There are three things to note about the way the apostle cites and employs this saying in 1 Corinthians 9.

First, in place of the word "laborer(s)" he has substituted the phrase, "those who proclaim the gospel." Perhaps this is because Paul has used the traditional word elsewhere with reference to "evil" (Phil 3:2) or "deceitful" (2 Cor 11:13) missionaries. In addition, the substitution helps him to register the point that Jesus' instruction applies in his own case no less than in the case of Jesus' disciples – for Paul wishes the Corinthians to think of him, above all, as the one who "proclaimed the gospel" to them (see, for example, 1 Cor 1:17; 9:16, 18; 15:1; 2 Cor 11:2).

Second, Paul conveys Jesus's words to the Corinthians as what "the Lord decreed." Here, as in the case of the divorce saying (1 Cor 7:10), Jesus is referred to as "the Lord." While the saying is introduced as something that the Lord has "decreed," in form it is not a regulation of any kind, but a simple statement. Yet in both Matthew and Luke its function is to support the directions that Jesus has given to those being sent out to preach:

Matthew 10—[9]Take no gold, or silver, or copper in your belts, [10]no bag for your journey, or two tunics, or sandals, or a staff; for laborers deserve their food.

Luke 10—[5]Whatever house you enter, first say, "Peace to this house!" [6]And if anyone is there who shares in peace, your peace will rest on that person; but if not, it will return to you. [7]Remain in the same house, eating and drinking whatever they provide, for the laborer deserves to be paid.

It is apparent that in both of these passages the saying, like the instructions, is directed to those whom Jesus is sending out. It is upon the missionaries that an obligation is laid. They are to devote their energies and time exclusively to their mission, and let others care for their daily needs – since "the laborer deserves to be paid." Of course, if missionaries adhere to this principle, an obligation will devolve as well upon those who receive them. Similarly, when Paul presents the saying as what "the Lord decreed" he is understanding it as directed to "those who proclaim the gospel." But he is no less aware of the obligation that this decree lays upon his congregations (1 Cor 9:12a, etc.).

Third, having cited the Lord's decree, Paul asserts that he has no intention of adhering to it when it comes to the Corinthians: "But I have made no use of any of these rights, nor am I writing this so that they may be applied in my case" (1 Cor 9:15a). We know that Paul was not opposed in principle to accepting material support from his congregations. While in Thessalonica he had received assistance "more than once" from the believers in Philippi (Phil 4:15–18), and he had also accepted help from "other churches" during his residency in

Corinth (2 Cor 11:8). But from the Corinthians he will accept no support, at least while he is staying in Corinth, and for that he is the object of their criticism. Perhaps they themselves have accused Paul of departing from the Lord's decree. Paul's response is to re-interpret that decree as a "right" which, for the sake of the gospel, he is free to give up (1 Cor 9:12, 15–18).

Echoes of the Sayings Tradition?

In the two passages we have considered so far Paul specifically identifies a saying as "the Lord's." The question we must now raise is whether there are also passages in which he is drawing on the sayings tradition even though he himself does not indicate that.

Whether there are echoes of Jesus' teachings in Paul's letters is very difficult to determine, and we can never arrive at a certain result. It is not enough to find places where Paul's ideas agree with sayings attributed to Jesus in the Synoptic Gospels. Agreement in ideas must be matched with at least some measure of agreement in wording. Moreover, in any given instance the agreements have to be with the *pre*-Synoptic form of the saying, insofar as that form can be reconstructed.

Two additional complicating factors come into play. First, some of the sayings in the Jesus tradition are similar in both form and content to teachings that had widespread currency in the first century, especially within the Jewish community. In such cases we cannot be sure whether Paul is echoing the Jesus tradition specifically, or some other. Second, the apostle may sometimes be echoing the teaching of Jesus without even realizing it himself. It is altogether possible that he knew some of Jesus' sayings not as *his* teaching, specifically, but simply as the teaching of the church.

One early twentieth-century scholar believed that he had

found almost one thousand allusions to Jesus' teachings in the Pauline letters! More recent and cautious scholars seldom suggest more than fifteen or twenty places where Paul may be echoing a saying from the Jesus tradition. But even in a number of these places, the similarities between a specific Pauline passage and a traditional saying are so general as to be outweighed by the differences. This would seem to be the case, for example, with Rom 13:8–10 (love one another and thus fulfill the law; compare Mark 12:31 and Matt 22:39), Rom 14:13 and 1 Cor 8:13 (put no hindrance in the way of a fellow believer; compare Mark 9:42 and parallels), Rom 15:1–2 (seek to please the neighbor rather than yourself; compare Mark 8:34–36; 10:42–45 and parallels), 1 Cor 10:27 (eat what your host provides; compare Luke 10:8), and 1 Thess 4:8 (beware of rejecting the authority of God; compare Luke 10:16).

In a few places, however, one can plausibly argue that Paul is drawing on a traditional saying of Jesus, even though he does not specifically invoke "the Lord's" authority. The clearest instances may be in Rom 12:14 and 14:14, which will need to be examined with some care. We may also take note, more briefly, of Rom 13:7 and 1 Cor 13:2. Since three of these fall within the same overall context in Romans, it will be useful to begin with some general remarks about that particular section of the letter.

Romans 12:1–15:13

The moral counsels and exhortations of Romans are concentrated within this section, although they presuppose and complement the argument of the preceding eleven chapters. In particular, they may be viewed as elaborating the apostle's earlier appeals that his readers be "dead to sin and alive to God in Christ Jesus" (6:11), and that they offer themselves up to God "as those who have been brought from death to life"

(6:13). This function of the exhortations in chapters 12–15 is clearly signalled by the way they are introduced (12:1–2):

¹Therefore, brothers and sisters, I implore you by the mercies of God to offer up your very selves as a live sacrifice, holy and acceptable to God, which is your reasonable worship. ²Do not let yourselves be conformed to this age, but allow yourselves to be transformed, with a renewed mind, so that you may search out what God's will is – what is good and acceptable and perfect. (Author's translation.)

The subject matter of the exhortations which follow is rather varied: use sober judgment (12:3–8), manifest genuine love (12:9–21), be good citizens (13:1–7), love the neighbor (13:8–10), cast off the works of darkness (13:11–14), and "put up with the failings of the weak" (14:1–15:13).

Romans 12:14

The topic in Rom 12:9–21 is given in the opening words, "Let love be genuine" (v. 9a). Paul writes first of how love should operate within the Christian community itself (vv. 10–13). Then in the following paragraph he indicates how love should shape the community's dealings with outsiders, including its enemies (vv. 14–21).

It is in the latter part of this passage that we may hear several echoes of the Jesus tradition. Of these, the likeliest comes in verse 14: "Bless those who persecute you; bless and do not curse them." The second part of this appeal repeats and reinforces the first part. With this repetition the decidedly radical character of the exhortation is accentuated. Rather than cursing one's persecutors – what one would presume to be the appropriate response (see, for example, Gen 12:3; 27:29) – one is called upon to bless them. In another letter the apostle says that he himself follows this rule: "when reviled, we bless" (1 Cor 4:12).

A similar admonition is attributed to Jesus in Luke 6:27–28, to which Matt 5:44 is parallel:

Luke 6—[27]Love your enemies, do good to those who hate you, [28]bless those who curse you, pray for those who abuse you.

Matthew 5—[44]Love your enemies and pray for those who persecute you.

In both of these instances the principal commandment, worded identically in Matthew and Luke, is to "love your enemies." In Luke, the three appeals that follow suggest what this should mean more particularly:

> Do good to those who hate you,
> bless those who curse you,
> pray for those who abuse you.

In Matthew, however, the principal commandment is followed only by the third of Luke's additional appeals. And rather than "those who abuse you" (Luke), Matthew has the more specific, "those who persecute you."

For whatever reason, the commandment to "love your enemies" is not present in any of the surviving Pauline letters. But it is quite possible that Paul's appeal in Rom 12:14 echoes a pre-Synoptic saying that was fairly similar in form to Luke 6:28, "bless those who curse you." Although the apostle's reference to "those who *persecute* you" aligns him in one respect with the Matthean parallel, the cursing theme is present in Paul's version no less than in Luke's, even though in a different way.

Apparently the same traditional saying is echoed in some other early Christian literature – for example, 1 Peter and the *Didache* ("Instruction"). The former is a New Testament writing which dates from either the late first or early second century. The latter is a collection of traditional Christian moral teachings which had attained its present form by the middle of the second century. As in Romans, there is no explicit association of the saying with Jesus.

1 Peter 3—⁹Do not repay evil for evil or reviling for reviling; but, on the contrary, repay with a blessing. (NRSV, modified.)

Didache 1—³Bless those who curse you and pray for your enemies; but fast for those who persecute you.

Neither of these passages is dependent on Matthew or Luke. Rather, as in those Gospels and in Romans, we are hearing echoes of the pre-Synoptic Jesus tradition. It is evident that various sayings from that tradition became a fixed part of the church's moral catechisms. Perhaps it was from these that Paul knew the saying about returning a curse with a blessing. In that case, he himself might have had no reason to think of it as a saying of Jesus.

It is sometimes suggested that Paul's subsequent appeal to "be at peace with all" (Rom 12:18, author's translation) is also drawn from the Jesus tradition. The apostle issues similar pleas in Rom 14:9 ("pursue what makes for peace"), 1 Thess 5:13 ("Be at peace among yourselves"), and 2 Cor 13:11 (simply, "be at peace"). According to Mark, Jesus urged the same: "Be at peace with one another" (9:50). However, unlike the commandment to "bless those who curse you," there is nothing radical, or even distinctively Christian, about the counsel to "be at peace." Such a counsel is present, for example, in Ps 34:14 ("seek peace, and pursue it"), a passage actually quoted in 1 Peter 3:11. It is in fact this psalmist's formulation which seems to lie behind the call for peace in Rom 14:19, and a similar one in Heb 12:14 (compare 2 Tim 2:22).

Romans 14:14

In Rom 14:1–15:13 Paul is offering counsel to the Christians of Rome about an issue that is threatening to divide their church.

It appears that the Jewish Christians of the city not only continue to observe certain food laws and holy days prescribed by
the Mosaic Law, but are calling the Gentile Christians to
account for not observing them. The Gentile Christians, for
their part, seem to be sharply critical of those in the church
who still feel bound by the law. (See, for example, 14:2–4,
10–12.) There are certain parallels between this situation and
the one that Paul had faced a few years before in his Corinthian
congregation (see 1 Cor 8:1–11:1). Indeed, the apostle's fundamental appeals to the Roman Christians are essentially the
same as his earlier appeals to the Corinthians.

As in 1 Corinthians, so here in Romans, Paul leaves no doubt
about his own views. On the one hand, he refers to those who
continue to adhere to the Jewish laws and rituals as "weak in
faith" (14:1). On the other hand, he regards those who realize
that they are not bound to those laws and rituals as "the strong,"
and explicitly identifies himself with them (15:1). For Paul,
Christians are not bound to the law but to their Lord (14:7–9).
Precisely for this reason, however, they are called to "walk in
love" toward one another (14:15), accepting one another even as
they themselves have been accepted by Christ (15:7). Paul is
fully aware that this places the greater responsibility upon the
strong, and so he charges them to "put up with the failings of the
weak" (15:1), doing nothing to make them fall (14:20–21).

It is in the apostle's comment about what is "clean" and
"unclean" (14:14) that we may be able to hear an echo of the
sayings tradition: "I know and am persuaded in the Lord Jesus
that nothing is unclean in itself; but it is unclean for anyone
who thinks it unclean." Some scholars believe that with the
introductory words, "I know and am persuaded in the Lord
Jesus," Paul is specifically identifying what follows as a saying
of Jesus. That is very unlikely, however. The introductory
words emphasize not the origin of the statement, but how
deeply Paul is committed to the truth of it (compare 14:5b,

22a). But even if this is not to be regarded as a direct citation of the Jesus tradition, does it echo it? Two passages from the Synoptic Gospels may be compared, and along with those a passage from the *Gospel of Thomas* (a second-century writing originating with Gnostic Christians).

Matthew 15—[10]Then [Jesus] called the crowd to him and said to them, "Listen and understand: [11]it is not what goes into the mouth that makes a person unclean, but what comes out of the mouth that makes one unclean." (NRSV, modified.)

Mark 7—[14]Then [Jesus] called the crowd again and said to them, "Listen to me, all of you, and understand: [15]there is nothing outside a person that by going in can make the person unclean, but the things that come out are what make one unclean." (NRSV, modified.)

Gospel of Thomas 14—Jesus said ... "what goes into your mouth will not make you unclean, but that which comes out of your mouth – it is that which will make you unclean."

The most distinctive of these three versions is Mark's, where the word "nothing" gives the saying a decidedly radical aspect. Consistent with this, in Mark – but not in Matthew or the *Gospel of Thomas* – readers are subsequently informed that Jesus had in effect "declared *all* foods clean" (Mark 7:19). Implicitly, at least, in its Marcan form the saying seems to be questioning one basic presupposition of the whole Jewish purificatory system.

The apostle's view of the matter is similarly radical: "*nothing* is unclean in itself" (Rom 14:14), "*everything* is indeed clean" (Rom 14:20). However, it would be premature to conclude that Paul was acquainted with a saying which was closer in content to Mark's version than to the versions in Matthew and the *Gospel of Thomas*. For one thing, there are some good reasons to think that the more moderate versions in Matthew and *Thomas* are the earlier. Mark may well have put a sharper edge on a saying which was less radical, at least in form, as it came to him. In addition, had such a radical saying been part of the pre-Synoptic Jesus tradition, it is hard to understand why there had been such conflict about clean and unclean foods in the early church (for example, the confront-ation between Peter and Paul in Antioch; Gal 2:11–14). One would suppose that a saying from Jesus in the Marcan form, had one been known, could have settled the question.

Even if Paul knew the saying in a form more like the one reflected in the Gospel of Matthew and the *Gospel of Thomas*, he obviously believed that it had far-reaching consequences. This is evident from his sweeping statements in Romans 14: "*nothing* is unclean in itself" (v. 14), "*everything* is indeed clean" (v. 20). The apostle's firm conviction in this matter makes his counsel to "the strong" all the more striking. Even though, like Paul, they are "persuaded in the Lord Jesus that nothing is unclean in itself," this is not the norm that is to govern their decisions about eating and drinking. Rather, that norm is to be Christ's death, through which they have been summoned to walk in love toward their weaker brothers and sisters (14:15; 15:1–3, 7–9a).

Romans 13:7

In Rom 13:1–7, as in Rom 14:1–15:13, Paul probably has in mind the special concerns of his Roman readers. He was either specifically aware or else presumed that, as residents of Caesar's own city, they would need counsel about paying taxes imposed by the government. It is known that during the period of time from which this letter must date there was increasing unrest, and not only among Jews and Christians, about the injustice of the imperial system of taxes. Paul's direction in the matter is given in verse 7:

Pay to all what is due them – taxes to whom taxes are due, revenue to whom revenue is due, respect to whom respect is due, honor to whom honor is due.

In this translation the English word "taxes" represents a Greek term that described taxes collected directly by imperial officers. The word "revenue" refers to indirect taxes, like harbor fees and duties on imports and exports. The collection of these two kinds of taxes, but especially of the latter, was attended by notorious abuses. Despite this, Paul says that all taxes should be paid.

It is often suggested that the apostle's instruction on this point reflects a saying from the Jesus tradition which is present in all three Synoptic Gospels (without any significant variation in wording):

Jesus said to them, "Pay to the emperor the things that are the emperor's, and to God the things that are God's." (Mark 12:17 [NRSV, modified]; see also Matt 22:21 and Luke 20:25.)

Here, as in Paul's letter, the general topic is paying taxes to Rome. Beyond this, the same Greek verb for "pay" is used in the traditional saying and in Paul's counsel, and the two formulations are equally pointed and succinct. Also, some interpreters believe that when Paul proceeds to call for "respect to whom respect is due" he is thinking of what one owes to God. If so, Rom 13:7 would echo the second part of the traditional saying as well as the first part.

If Paul did in fact formulate his counsel about taxes with the traditional saying in mind, then it is quite remarkable how freely he has employed it in Rom 13:7. In the saying itself the call to pay to God what belongs to God goes quite beyond the question that Jesus had been asked. The emphasis is thereby shifted away from Caesar's claim to God's. Thus, the saying as the apostle would have received it spoke primarily of what one owes to God. Even if this point is echoed in Rom 13:7, as some believe, the echo is very faint. Clearly, Paul's main concern is with what one owes to Caesar.

1 Corinthians 13:2

Paul's Corinthian congregation was divided over the matter of speaking in tongues. The apostle's specific instructions about that come in 1 Corinthians 14, but already in the two preceding chapters he is laying the groundwork. First, in chapter 12 the church is portrayed as the body of Christ, whose members have diverse gifts and are therefore wholly interdependent. Then in the classic discourse of chapter 13, love is presented as a "more excellent way" than any particular spiritual gift. Finally, in chapter 14 the apostle indicates that following love's way will require the reordering of some priorities and procedures when the Corinthians assemble for their worship.

The discourse on love is opened with a series of three parallel sentences, each one including the refrain, "but [if I] do not have love ... " (vv. 1–3). Some interpreters believe that in the second of these three (v. 2) Paul is drawing, in part, from the Jesus tradition:

And if I have prophetic powers, and understand all mysteries and all knowledge, and if I have all faith, so as to remove mountains, but do not have love, I am nothing.

The reference here to having "all faith, so as to remove mountains" is reminiscent of a saying known from the Synoptic Gospels (Matt 17:20; 21:21; Mark 11:22–23). In addition, the idea of moving a mountain – without any mention of faith – occurs in two of the sayings of Jesus contained in the *Gospel of Thomas* (48 and 106). The Synoptic version most comparable with 1 Cor 13:2 is Matt 17:20 (the versions in Matthew 21 and Mark both have a mountain being "thrown into the sea"). Having explained to his disciples that they had been unable to help an epileptic man because they lacked the necessary faith, Jesus then says:

For truly I tell you, if you have faith the size of a mustard seed, you will say to this mountain, "Move from here to there," and it will move; and nothing will be impossible for you.

While it might seem obvious that some form of this saying was known to Paul, two points give pause.

(1) We are dealing here with a proverbial expression which was widely known and used in Paul's day. To speak of "moving a mountain" was to speak of doing something which to all appearances is impossible. This means that Paul could have been familiar with the expression quite apart from his knowledge of a saying from the Jesus tradition. It is true, however, that the notion of "faith" being able to move a mountain is present only in the Synoptic Gospels and Paul. Does this not show that the apostle is echoing a pre-Synoptic saying in which that connection had been made? Not necessarily, because a second point must also be considered.

(2) While the saying as found in Matt 17:20 is the one most like Paul's remark in 1 Cor 13:2, it is likely that Luke 17:5–6 preserves it in an earlier form. If so, it is in Luke that we come closest to a *pre*-Synoptic saying that Paul might have known. But instead of a mountain, the Lucan version refers to a mulberry tree!

[5]The apostles said to the Lord, "Increase our faith!" [6]The Lord replied, "If you had faith the size of a mustard seed, you could say to this mulberry tree, 'Be uprooted and planted in the sea,' and it would obey you."

Despite this complicated situation, one point can be made with confidence. If a saying from the Jesus tradition does lie behind 1 Cor 13:2, the apostle has felt quite free to employ it in his own way. The saying had called for faith and had emphasized its astounding power. But Paul is appealing for love, and insists that nothing exceeds it in importance.

Special Cases

Before this chapter is brought to a close, some consideration must be given to 1 Cor 14:37, 2 Cor 12:8–9, and 1 Thess 4:15–17.

Little need be said about 2 Cor 12:8–9, indeed only enough to suggest why it falls outside the scope of the present discussion. After mentioning a "thorn in the flesh" by which he was tormented (very likely some chronic illness), Paul says:

[8]Three times I appealed to the Lord about this, that it would leave me, [9]but he said to me, "My grace is sufficient for you, for power is made perfect in weakness."

This is a "saying of Jesus" only in a very special sense. Paul himself identifies it as a pronouncement that he has received from the risen Lord. He does not cite it as part of the "public teaching" of the earthly Jesus. This is not a saying drawn from the tradition, but a divine oracle spoken directly to Paul.

The apostle's statement in 1 Cor 14:37 opens the concluding paragraph of his directions about the proper ordering of worship.

[37]Anyone who claims to be a prophet, or to have spiritual powers, must acknowledge that what I am writing to you is a command of the Lord.

It has been suggested, occasionally, that the "command of the Lord" to which Paul refers here is some specific saying of Jesus. That is very unlikely, however, because nothing in the preceding discussion has any convincing parallel in the Jesus traditions as we know those from the Synoptic Gospels.

In this instance, the illuminating parallels are with Paul's statement as a whole, and they are not in the Jesus tradition but earlier in this very letter. Upon concluding a discussion of true and false wisdom, Paul had claimed to "have the mind of Christ" (2:16). And upon concluding his counsels about marriage, he had claimed to "have the Spirit of God" (7:40). In both places he is emphasizing the special insight and authority he believes to be his as an apostle. Now, upon concluding his introductions about worship, he makes a similar claim. Whoever is truly a "spiritual" person (many in Corinth boasted of that status) will recognize that what he has written comes to them with the authority that only the Lord can bestow.

The most problematic of these special cases is 1 Thess 4:15–17, which occurs in a passage where Paul is writing about the expected return of Christ. The Thessalonians are concerned that those in their congregation who have already died may not share equally in salvation with those who will still be alive. In assuring them that this is definitely not the case, Paul says:

> [15]For this we declare to you by the word of the Lord, that we who are alive, who are left until the coming of the Lord, will by no means precede those who have died. [16]For the Lord himself, with a cry of command, with the archangel's call and with the sound of God's trumpet, will descend from heaven, and the dead in Christ will rise first. [17]Then we who are alive, who are left, will be caught up in the clouds together with them to meet the Lord in the air ...

Three related questions have to be faced here. Does "by the word of the Lord' (v. 15a) mean "by *citing a saying* of the Lord"? If so, where is Paul conveying that saying, in verse 15b or in verses 16–17? And where can we locate that saying within the Jesus tradition known to us?

Some interpreters believe that Paul is indeed referring to a specific saying, or perhaps to a specific group of sayings which provided teaching about the last days. They find this reflected in verses 16–17, with which they compare, especially, Matt 24:29–31. But one of the difficulties is that the end-time imagery which is common to Paul and the Synoptics is found in many Jewish sources as well. It need not derive specifically from the Jesus tradition. Thus, others have suggested – not very persuasively – that Paul is citing a saying otherwise unknown, on which verse 15b could in fact be based.

But if Paul is not actually drawing on the Jesus tradition, why does he say that he is speaking "by the word of the Lord"? In his Greek Bible exactly this phrase was used with reference to prophetic oracles (see 1 Kings 13:1, 2, 5, 32; 20:35; Sirach 48:3). Perhaps, then, Paul means that he is conveying an oracle which has been formulated *"in the name* of the Lord" by some Christian prophet – or even by himself (compare 2 Cor 12:9). Alternatively, as with his reference to "a command of the Lord" in 1 Cor 14:37, he could mean that he is speaking *"with the authority* of the Lord."

Concluding Observations

Our survey has confirmed that Paul both knew and on occasion cited sayings we know to have been part of the Jesus tradition. Beyond this, several concluding observations are in order.

First, we have noted that in those places where Paul explicitly cites a saying, he refers to its source as "the Lord," not as "Jesus." We should not suppose, however, that the apostle himself would have found such a distinction very meaningful. The sayings of Jesus which he knows from the tradition, he knows as the words of the Lord. For him, those are in principle no different from the words of the Lord that he can convey (as in 1 Cor 14 and 1 Thess 4) because he has "the mind of Christ" (1 Cor 2:16). Whether the Lord's words have come to him through the tradition or "by revelation" (see Gal 1:16), Paul is confident that it is Christ who is speaking through him (2 Cor 13:3).

Second, there are indications that Paul knew more of the traditional sayings of Jesus than he actually cites. Specific echoes of those are difficult to identify, however, and impossible to confirm. Moreover, echoes do not necessarily represent intentional allusions, and whether Paul's readers would have recognized such allusions has to be left as an open question. Indeed, it is significant that they remain *allusions*; the Lord's authority is not specifically invoked.

Third, Paul accords special authority to the words of the Lord. This is particularly clear in 1 Cor 7:10, 12, 25, where he carefully distinguishes between his own opinions and the Lord's decrees. It is therefore all the more striking that Paul does not hesitate to interpret and apply those decrees in his own way, and even to depart from them if he believes the situation warrants. We have seen this happening not only where he may be echoing Jesus' teaching (Rom 13:7; 14:14; 1 Cor 13:2), but even where he has specifically called on the Lord's authority (1 Cor 7:10–11, 15 and 1 Cor 9:14, 15). Paul has not turned the sayings of Jesus into a "new law."

A final observation is especially important. The apostle nowhere employs a traditional saying of Jesus to help present or support his own most basic affirmations about the gospel. Those are presented and supported primarily with reference to Jesus' death and resurrection. Paul does not understand his apostolic task to be merely handing on Jesus' teachings, or interpreting and applying them. He understands his task to be, above all, proclaiming Jesus himself, as God's agent for reconciliation (2 Cor 5:18–20).

Chapter 4

Jesus in Paul's Gospel

Introduction

Where Paul summarizes or otherwise identifies the content of his preaching it is almost always with reference to Jesus.

Rom 15:19—From Jerusalem and as far around as Illyricum I have fully proclaimed the good news of Christ.

1 Cor 2:2—For I decided to know nothing among you except Jesus Christ, and him crucified.

1 Cor 15:12—Christ is proclaimed as raised from the dead ...

2 Cor 1:19—For the Son of God, Jesus Christ, whom we proclaimed among you ...

2 Cor 4:5—We proclaim Jesus Christ as Lord ...

2 Cor 11:4—For if someone comes and proclaims another Jesus than the one we proclaimed ...

Gal 1:15–16—God ... was pleased to reveal his Son to me so that I might proclaim him among the Gentiles.

Gal 3:1b—It was before your eyes that Jesus Christ was publicly exhibited as crucified!

Phil 1:18—Christ is proclaimed in every way, whether out of false motives or true; and in that I rejoice.

When these and other representative statements are taken into account, it becomes apparent that the apostle proclaims Jesus both as the crucified Messiah (see especially, 1 Cor 1:18–2:5) and as the risen and living Lord (Rom 6:9; 1 Cor 6:14; 15:12). For him, as in the creedal statements he sometimes employs (1 Cor 15:3–5; 1 Thess 4:14), Jesus' death and resurrection belong inseparably together. And in addition, he is confident that Jesus will soon return, that "the day of the Lord" is not far off (Rom 13:11–12a; 1 Thess 1:9–10; 5:2). Thus, Jesus according to Paul is a uniquely "three-dimensional" figure – uniquely so, because the dimensions are traced not in space but in time. In the Pauline letters we are presented with a Jesus who was crucified and resurrected (past), who even now remains the crucified and resurrected one (present), and who will come again (future).

For the apostle, to preach this Christ is to give voice to *the gospel*. First of all, therefore, we will need to take account of what Paul understands the "gospel" to be. Next we shall examine his three-dimensional presentation of Jesus. That, in turn, will show us the importance of considering how, in Paul's view, Jesus continues to be present within the community of faith.

"The Gospel" in Paul's Letters

In the New Testament itself, the word "gospel" is never used with reference to a document. It was at least the middle of the second century before the term was applied to the writings that we know as the four "Gospels." The Greek noun (*euangelion* – literally, "good news") occurs far more often in the Pauline letters than in any other part of the New Testament. It had been used originally of the oral reporting of good news, and then eventually of the report itself. This is the meaning it has, for example, in the Greek version of 2 Sam 4:10 (the report, delivered to David, about Saul's death). There is one example of this everyday sense in Paul's letters, when he mentions the "good report" that Timothy has brought to him about the congregation in Thessalonica (1 Thess 3:6, author's translation). Elsewhere, however, Paul employs the noun with reference to the "good news" of salvation.

Paul seems to have been the first to use the noun in this

religious sense. In this he was perhaps influenced by the Greek version of the book of Isaiah, where forms of the related verb, "to 'gospel,'" occur in several of the salvation oracles of chapters 40–66. For example, according to Isa 52:7 (which is echoed by Paul in Rom 10:15) God is present to Israel "as one who 'gospels' news of peace, as one who 'gospels' good tidings" concerning salvation (author's translation). Again, in Isa 40:9–11 the word of the one who "gospels" to Zion is that the Lord himself is coming with strength, and to tend his flock as a shepherd. (See also Isa 60:6 and 61:1.)

Paul's statement about the gospel in Rom 1:16–17 is quite in accord with these prophetic oracles:

[16]For I am not ashamed of the gospel; it is the power of God for salvation to everyone who has faith, to the Jew first and also to the Greek. [17]For in it the righteousness of God is revealed through faith for faith ...

Clearly, Paul understands the gospel to be something much more than just *a message* about God, or Christ, or salvation. He is thinking of it first of all as *an event* – specifically, as the event of God's own powerful, saving presence and activity (compare especially, Isa 40:9–11). It is delivered not just "in word" but also "in power" (1 Thess 1:5). It is not just a recital of ideas, but the "revealing" of God's righteousness "through faith for faith." This means, in turn, that "faith" is more than the passive reception of a message. For Paul, "believing" the gospel means "obeying" it. In Rom 10:16 these two words are used interchangeably: "But not all have *obeyed* the gospel; for Isaiah says, 'Lord, who has *believed* our message?'" Because the gospel discloses God's righteousness (Rom 1:16–17), obeying the gospel means allowing God's righteousness to rule in one's life (thus, Rom 6:15–19).

The apostle sometimes refers to "the gospel of God" (for example, Rom 1:1; 15:16), and elsewhere to "the gospel of Christ" (for example, Rom 15:19; 1 Cor 9:12). There is no difference in meaning, since for Paul it is through Christ that God's own power and righteousness are operative for salvation (for example, 1 Cor 1:24, 30). This is why his preaching of the gospel of God is nothing else than the preaching of Christ.

Jesus the Crucified Messiah

What Paul says about his preaching in Corinth and Galatia seems to have been true of his preaching in general; it was above all the proclamation of "Jesus Christ, and him crucified" (1 Cor 2:2; Gal 3:1b; see also 1 Cor 1:23; Gal 6:14). It is therefore no change in subject when, after a reference to "the gospel" (1 Cor 1:17), he proceeds to comment on "the word of the cross" (1 Cor 1:18, author's translation). This is confirmed by the parallelism of Rom 1:16 and 1 Cor 1:18: in Romans the gospel is described as "the power of God for salvation," and in 1 Corinthians the word of the cross is described as "the power of God" for "those who are being saved." Thus, on occasion he refers to "the cross" where he might just as well have written, "the gospel" (Gal 5:11; 6:12; Phil 3:18).

This identification of the gospel with "the word of the cross" should not be taken for granted. For one thing, it is quite distinctively Pauline, found nowhere else in the New Testament. Moreover, the preaching of "Jesus Christ and him crucified" must have struck Paul's hearers as a very strange kind of "gospel." Crucifixion was recognized throughout the ancient world as an unusually cruel and painful method of execution. It had been adopted by the Romans from the Phoenicians and Persians, and was ordinarily employed only when the condemned was a slave or a foreigner. The Jewish historian, Josephus, called it "the most wretched of deaths." His judgment was shared even by Roman writers – like Tacitus, who termed it "disgraceful," and Cicero who described it as "savage." How, then, can Paul dare to be offering "good news," if he proclaims only a *crucified* Messiah?

The first step in answering this question is to observe that Paul shows little interest in the historical circumstances of Jesus' death, apart from the fact that it was by crucifixion. He knew of a nighttime betrayal (1 Cor 11:23) but he does not identify the betrayer. He says nothing about the arrest itself, what charges were brought against Jesus, before whom he was tried, or how the trial was conducted. Neither does he mention the time or place of Jesus' death, or who was with him, or any final words he may have spoken. And while Paul knows of an entombment (1 Cor 15:4; Rom 6:4), he does not indicate where it was or who was responsible for it.

Nor does he seek to assign a historical cause for Jesus' death. If Paul himself wrote the passage in 1 Thessalonians where "the Jews" are blamed for it (2:14–15), that is as close as he ever comes; but there are good reasons to think that the passage is from a later hand. And when he says elsewhere that "the rulers of this age ... crucified the Lord of glory" (1 Cor 2:8), he is probably not thinking of political authorities. That reference is more likely to the kind of cosmic powers which, he says, will finally be subject to Christ and to God (see 1 Cor 15:24).

Jesus' Death as Faithful Obedience

Paul's overall indifference to the historical causes and circumstances of Jesus' death is not hard to explain. For him, Jesus' death is not just something that happened "once upon a time" in history. He interprets it as an *act of God*, as a *saving* event of cosmic proportions and timeless significance. This is just as much the case when the apostle refers to Jesus' giving up of *himself* to death (Gal 2:20; see also 1 Cor 11:24), as when he says that *God* gave him up (Rom 3:24–25; 4:25; 8:32), because Jesus' self-giving is nothing else than his obedience to the will of God (Gal 1:3–4). Jesus' death is also characterized as an act of obedience in the hymn of Philippians 2 (vv. 6–8). The descriptive words, "even death on a cross" serve to emphasize that, and may well be the apostle's own interpretive addition to the hymn.

Another specific reference to Jesus' obedience occurs in Rom 5:12–21, where Paul contrasts it with the disobedience of the first and representative human being, "Adam." Summing up (vv. 18–19), the apostle writes:

> [18]Therefore, just as one man's trespass led to condemnation for all, so one man's act of righteousness leads to justification and life for all. [19]For just as by the one man's disobedience the many were made sinners, so by the one man's obedience the many will be made righteous.

Given the context, the "obedience" (v. 19), or "act of righteousness" (v. 18), to which Paul refers can only be Jesus' death. That has been the apostle's subject in Rom 5:6–11, and it is still very much in view in Rom 6:1–11.

There is no other place where Paul refers directly to Jesus' obedience. On occasion, however, it is just possible that he is thinking of Jesus' "faith" (or perhaps "faithfulness"). The places in question are Rom 3:22, 26; Gal 2:16 (twice), 20; 3:22; and Phil 3:9. According to most translations, including the NRSV, Paul's reference in each of these passages is to having "faith *in* Jesus" (thus, Rom 3:26; or "in Jesus Christ," Rom 3:22, etc.). But in each instance the NRSV also provides an alternative translation, which takes the reference to be to Jesus' *own* faith. Should this second interpretation be correct, as some interpreters have argued, what would Paul have in mind? Probably not the general "faith in God" by which Jesus lived his life and conducted his ministry. As we have seen, the apostle seems to have paid little attention to these. More likely, Paul would be thinking in particular of that faithful obedience to God's will which led Jesus, finally, to the cross (see especially, Rom 3:21–26 and Gal 2:19–21).

Jesus' Death as a Saving Event

Paul proclaims the word of the cross as "good news" because he is convinced that Jesus died "for us (all)" (see especially, Rom 5:8; 8:32; 2 Cor 5:14–15; Gal 3:13; 1 Thess 5:10). Sometimes he says, "for our sins" (1 Cor 15:3; Gal 1:4; compare Rom 4:25; 5:6). In these and the few other places where he uses the plural, "sins," the apostle appears to be echoing traditional language. More often he refers to "sin," using the singular form. This accords with his view that sin is a *power*, whose tyrannical rule alienates humanity from God and disrupts all other relationships. Sin rules by "deceiving" human beings into supposing that they can live out of their own finite resources (see Rom 7:11). Sin means the refusal to "honor" (literally, "glorify") and "give thanks" to the God from whom all life comes, and in whose service life finds its meaning (Rom 1:21, with reference to Gentiles; Rom 2:23, with reference to Jews). Paul develops and illustrates this point in Rom 1:18–3:20, and then sums it up in Rom 3:22b–23: "there is no distinction, since all have sinned and fall short of the glory of God." The apostle insists no less, however, that all are the beneficiaries of God's saving grace. This is his theme in Rom 3:21–8:39.

Paul's understanding of salvation follows from his understanding of sin. The plight of humankind is to be tyrannized by sin's rule, and thereby alienated from God and one's own true humanity. Accordingly, salvation means deliverance from sin's power, being put right with God, and being restored to an authentically human existence. These are precisely the kinds of images that Paul employs when he writes about the salvation effected by Christ's death. He has drawn some, or perhaps most of them from the tradition, and they overlap in meaning. The apostle shows no interest in drawing sharp distinctions or systematizing them (see, for example, 1 Cor

1:30), and it is better not to attempt this for him. A few exemplary passages will make the point.

Romans 3:21–26. The dominant image here is that of being *put right* ("justified"; see also 4:25; 5:1–11; 8:32–34; Gal 2:19–21). This has in view a restored relationship with God, which comes about through "[God's] grace as a gift" (v. 24a). But in identifying God's grace with Jesus' death, two further images are introduced: "the *redemption* that it is Christ Jesus, whom God put forward as a *sacrifice of atonement* by his blood" (vv. 24b–25). Here "redemption" is used metaphorically for release from sin's power – as when, for a specified sum, the freedom of a slave or prisoner of war was purchased. In other places, too, Paul uses this or a related image to describe what Christ's death accomplished (for example, Rom 6:6; 1 Cor 6:20a and 7:23a; Gal 1:4; 3:13). To call it, further, a "sacrifice of atonement" is to borrow an image from the Jewish sacrificial system. With this it is suggested that the people's sins have been transferred to Christ, and his innocence to them (see also 1 Cor 5:7).

Romans 5:1–11. Here, too, Paul describes Jesus' death as *putting one right* with God (vv. 1, 9). This he now enriches with a second image, that of *being reconciled* to God (vv. 9–11). It is not just that a broken relationship has been restored. "Reconciliation" means, in a quite positive sense, having "peace with God" (v. 1).

2 Corinthians 5:14–21. As in Romans 5, Paul views Jesus' death (vv. 14–15 – quoted above, p. 35) as bringing *reconciliation* with God (vv. 18–20). Also, as in Romans 3, he suggests that Jesus' death makes atonement for sins. Here, however, the formulation – probably echoing a traditional statement – is more striking: "The one who knew no sin he made to be sin for us, that in him we might become the righteousness of God" (v. 21, author's translation). Rom 8:3–4 is comparable:

[3]For God has done what the law, weakened by the flesh, could not do: by sending his own Son in the likeness of sinful flesh, and to deal with sin, he condemned sin in the flesh, [4]so that the just requirement of the law might be fulfilled in us, who walk not according to the flesh but according to the Spirit.

Some interpreters believe that in these passages Paul is echoing Isaiah 53, where the prophet describes the innocent, and thus redemptive, suffering of God's "servant" (perhaps a metaphor for the people of Israel):

> [5]But he was wounded for our transgressions,
>   crushed for our iniquities;
> upon him was the punishment that made us whole,
>   and by his bruises we are healed ...
> [6]and the Lord has laid on him
>   the iniquity of us all ...
> [11]The righteous one, my servant, shall make many righteous,
>   and he shall bear their iniquities ...
> [12]he bore the sin of many,
>   and made intercession for the transgressors.

But whether or not Paul thinks of Jesus as this suffering servant, there is no doubt that he views Jesus' suffering and death as redemptive. Through the cross, sin's power has been broken and righteousness has been bestowed. Further, Paul declares that with Jesus' death "*all* have died" (v. 14) in order that they might live "no longer for themselves, but for [Christ] who died and was raised for them" (v. 15). What this means is best seen in Romans and Galatians.

Romans 6:1–7:6; Galatians 2:19b; 5:24; 6:14. In both Romans and Galatians Paul writes, rather daringly, of being *crucified with Christ*. Baptism into Christ's death, he says, means the "crucifixion" of one's old, sin-dominated self (Rom 6:3–4, 5–7). This metaphor shows up again in Gal 2:19b, where the first person singular is meant to include all believers: "I have been crucified with Christ."

The metaphor of crucifixion appears twice more in Galatians. Paul writes that "those who belong to Christ Jesus have crucified the flesh with its passions and desires" (5:24). Then, in concluding the letter, he declares that "the world has been crucified to me, and I to the world" (6:14). For him, this crucifixion of "the flesh" and "the world" does not only mean putting away evil desires and temptations. It means nothing less than the death of the old self (as in Rom 6:1–11 and Gal 2:19–21), and thus deliverance from sin's tyrannical power (see especially, Rom 6:12–14 and 7:5–6).

But there is more. According to Paul, as one dies to sin's rule one comes *"alive* to God in Christ Jesus" (Rom 6:11). Through Christ's death believers have been empowered to "walk in newness of life" (Rom 6:4). Having been set under the rule of grace, they are bound over to righteousness (Rom 6:17–18). With such affirmations we have arrived at the very heart of Paul's gospel, where we are confronted with a profound paradox. The "word of the cross" is the good news that Christ's death means life for those who are baptized into his death (Rom 6:1–11). It is the good news that to be crucified with Christ is to be alive with him to God (Gal 2:19–21). It is the good news that God's saving power is at work precisely in the weakness of the cross.

The Strange Power of the Cross

How can Paul describe Jesus, the crucified Messiah, as God's "wisdom" and God's "power" (1 Cor 1:24)? How can he claim that the cross exposes the world's "wisdom" as foolishness (1 Cor 1:20–25a) and the world's "strength" as weakness (1 Cor 1:25b, 26–29)? How can Jesus' death bring life? What kind of strange, saving power is operative through the cross?

We can summarize these questions by posing yet another. According to Paul, what characterized Jesus' faithful "act of righteousness" which took him to the cross? About this the

apostle leaves us in no doubt. Jesus' death was an act of love
(*agape*), selfless and absolutely unconditional. The most compelling statement of this stands in Rom 5:6, 8, following an
assurance that "hope does not disappoint us, because God's
love has been poured into our hearts through the Holy Spirit"
(v. 5). Continuing, Paul writes further of the source and character of this love:

[6]For while we were still weak, at the right time Christ died for the
ungodly ... [8]But God proves his love for us in that while we were still
sinners Christ died for us.

Christ's death "proves" God's love because he laid down his
life for those who, by any worldly standard, remain unworthy
of such a gift (the "weak," the "ungodly," "sinners," vv. 6, 8;
and those hostile to God, v. 10). Because there is no reckoning
of who are worthy to receive it and who are not, the reconciling
power of God's love, like its scope, is unlimited. This is a
power which in the eyes of the world remains forever strange,
because it is demonstrated in what the world can only count as
weakness – in a love which is given without any conditions,
and which therefore appears to be utterly naive, absolutely
vulnerable.

It is this unconditional and therefore sovereign love which
constitutes God's grace, and which is Paul's main topic
throughout Rom 3:21–8:39. At the close of this section of the
letter, summing up, he asks: "If God is for us, who is against
us?" (Rom 8:31b). Answering his own question, he affirms that
nothing "in all creation will be able to separate us from the
love of God in Christ Jesus our Lord" (Rom 8:39). And here,
too, this reconciling power of God's love is understood to be
disclosed in Christ's death (see Rom 8:32). The same is true in
2 Cor 5:14: "For the love of Christ lays claim to us, since we
have come to the conviction that one has died for all" (NRSV,
modified). Here the apostle is thinking very specifically of the
power of this love to effect reconciliation (see 2 Cor 5:18–20).

The association of Christ's love with his death is also present in Gal 2:19–21, where the first person singular is meant to include all believers:

[19]For through the law I died to the law, so that I might live to God. I have been crucified with Christ; [20]and it is no longer I who live, but it is Christ who lives in me. [21]And the life I now live in the flesh I live by faith in the Son of God, who loved me and gave himself for me.

While crucifixion with Christ means being no longer oriented to worldly claims and values (Gal 5:24; 6:14), it does not remove believers from the world. They continue to live "in the flesh" (v. 21) – that is, in "the present evil age" (1:4). The difference is, they have now been set free from their bondage to this age, and live "by faith in the Son of God." Paul means, specifically, that they live by faith in the saving power of the love disclosed in Christ's death. This holds true even if one accepts the alternative translation, "by *the* faith *of* the Son of God." In either case, Paul is defining the faith by which one lives with reference to Christ's self-giving love on the cross.

In this same passage, faith is also defined with reference to the saving power of Christ's *living presence*: "it is no longer I who live, but it is Christ who lives in me" (compare Phil 1:21, "For to me, living is Christ ... "). Elsewhere in Galatians the apostle writes of God's sending "the Spirit of his Son into our hearts" (4:6). There are similar statements in Rom 8:9–11, where the indwelling "Spirit of Christ" is said to bring righteousness and life (vv. 9b–10). In Romans 8, it is clearly the Spirit of the *resurrected* Christ of which Paul is thinking (see v. 11).

Jesus the Risen Lord

Even though the cross is at the very center of Paul's witness to Christ, it is always understood to be the cross of the one whom God raised from the dead. This is nicely exhibited in

1 Corinthians. In opening the letter Paul insists that he has preached nothing in Corinth "except Jesus Christ, and him crucified" (2:2). And in closing the letter he argues that "if Christ has not been raised, then our proclamation has been in vain ... " (15:14).

Modern readers approach this topic of Jesus' resurrection with many questions. Did it actually happen? If so, when and under what circumstances? To whom did the risen Jesus first appear, and where? What exactly did he do and say? When and how did he depart? We shall be disappointed, however, if we expect to find answers to such questions in Paul's letters. The apostle's various statements about Jesus' resurrection are not intended to answer historical, or even theological questions about it. He simply presupposes that Jesus was raised from the dead, and seems confident that his readers share his conviction.

"Easter" According to Paul

Paul's most extensive remarks about Jesus' resurrection come in chapter 15 of 1 Corinthians. Jesus' resurrection is not, however, the real focus of this chapter. Paul's subject is the resurrection of the dead which, in his view, will occur at the close of history. It is in urging the Corinthians not to abandon hope for the coming resurrection, that he appeals to their belief in Jesus' own resurrection: "Now if Christ is proclaimed as raised from the dead, how can some of you say there is no resurrection of the dead?" (v. 12).

The apostle opens his argument by citing a tradition that he had received and then handed on to the Corinthians:

[3]that Christ died for our sins in accordance with the scriptures, [4]and that he was buried, and that he was raised on the third day in accordance with the scriptures, [5]and that he appeared to Cephas, then to the twelve.

With the citation of this tradition, Paul comes closer than he does anywhere else to locating Jesus' resurrection in time ("on the third day"). Even here, however, he is not presenting the resurrection simply as a public event in world history, however grand. Rather, he is presenting it as an act of God, an event whose significance transcends both time and space. Is this why he says nothing about the discovery of an empty tomb? Or did he not know of any such story? Scholars are divided on this point. He does, however, enumerate five distinct appearances of the resurrected Jesus to his followers:

1. To Cephas (Peter), v. 5
2. To the twelve (disciples), v. 5
3. To more than 500 believers (all at once), v. 6
4. To James, the Lord's brother, v. 7
5. To all the apostles, v. 7

It is obvious that various traditions about Jesus' resurrection appearances were circulating in the church. These happen to be the ones known to Paul. But according to Matthew there had been just two resurrection appearances: one to Mary Magdalene and "the other Mary" as they left the tomb (Matt 28:9–10), and a second to the disciples in Galilee (28:16–20). According to Luke there had also been two: one to Cleopas and an unnamed companion at Emmaus (Luke 24:13–35), and a second to the disciples in Jerusalem (24:36–43).

According to John, chapter 20, Jesus appeared three times: first, to Mary Magdalene near the tomb (John 20:11–18); second, to the disciples in Jerusalem, with Thomas absent (20:19–25); third, to the disciples (again in Jerusalem), with Thomas present (20:26–29). (Nothing is said about an appearance to Peter and the beloved disciple, even though they are at the empty tomb, 20:3–10). In chapter 21 of John, probably a later addition, there is yet another appearance to the disciples, this one in Galilee. Finally, in Mark 16:9–20, which is almost certainly a late addition to that Gospel, there are again three appearances: one to Mary Magdalene at the tomb (Mark 16:9); a second to "two of them, as they were walking into the country" (v. 12); and a third to "the eleven ... as they were sitting at the table" (v. 14).

In distinction from these Gospel accounts, Paul provides no narrative details with his list of appearances. There is no indication of when these appearances took place, or over how long a period of time (except that the 500 believers were visited all "at one time," v. 6). And there is no mention at all of the places or circumstances. Perhaps most striking, however, is Paul's bold move in v. 8. There he lists his own encounter with Christ at Damascus (see Gal 1:16–17 and 1 Cor 9:1) as still another of Jesus' resurrection appearances!

In accord with his main concern in this chapter, Paul uses a special form of the Greek verb, "to raise" (vv. 4, 12, 13, 16, 17, 20). The ordinary past tense would mean simply that "once upon a time Christ was raised from the dead." But the tense Paul uses suggests more, that "Christ *has been raised* from the dead and *continues to be present* as the risen One." And what is this continuing significance, according to Paul? In considering this, it will be useful to survey the apostle's other affirmations about Jesus as the risen Lord.

Other Affirmations about Jesus' Resurrection

Among Paul's letters, only the short note to Philemon lacks some explicit reference to Jesus as the risen One. The specific form and content of these references vary from passage to passage. In some places the apostle follows fairly closely the wording of traditional affirmations. That is the case in 1 Cor 15:3–5, and also, for example, in Rom 1:3–4; 4:24–25; 8:34; 10:9, and 1 Thess 1:10; 4:14. In other places statements about Jesus' resurrection are worded in a more distinctly Pauline way. Among these, Rom 14:9 and 2 Cor 4:10–11, 14;

13:4 are particularly noteworthy. When all of these passages are taken into account, several points stand out especially.

First, the apostle's affirmations about the risen Lord are as much about God as about Jesus (see especially, Rom 4:24, 8:11; 2 Cor 4:14; Gal 1:1). He consistently presents Jesus' resurrection as an act of God, as a manifestation of God's power. Paul avoids saying that Jesus *rose* from the dead, as if on his own (such an expression occurs only in 1 Thess 4:14). He uses either a passive form of the verb, Christ "was raised," etc. (for example, Rom 6:4; 1 Cor 15:4; 2 Cor 5:15), or else he makes it clear in some other way that *God* is the one who has raised Jesus from the dead (for example, 1 Cor 6:14; 15:15; 1 Thess 1:10). This is in keeping with the traditional Jewish description of God as "one who raises the dead" (reflected, for example, in Rom 4:17 and 2 Cor 1:9).

Second, there are only two places where Paul refers to Jesus' resurrection without referring also to Jesus' death (1 Cor 6:14; 2 Cor 4:14). Often the reference is to Jesus who "was raised from the dead" (as in Rom 4:24; 6:4; 8:11; 1 Cor 15:12; Gal 1:1). Another formulation is the two-part statement that Jesus "died and was raised" (Rom 8:34; 1 Cor 15:3–4). Typically Pauline variations of this two-part form are found in Rom 14:9, "Christ died and lived again," and 2 Cor 13:4, "He was crucified in weakness, but lives by the power of God."

The point is this: Paul does not understand Jesus' resurrection to have canceled out or to have overcome Jesus' death. In Paul's eyes, Jesus the risen Lord is still Jesus the crucified Messiah. It is not Jesus as he was known before "Good Friday" who has been resurrected, but the Jesus who died upon the cross. Thus, the same special verb tense that he uses with reference to the resurrection is sometimes used with reference to the crucifixion (in 1 Cor 1:23; 2:2 and Gal 3:1). For him, Jesus *continues* to be present as the crucified One. It is significant that the cross – not, for example, the empty tomb – is the central symbol of Paul's gospel.

A third point is closely related to the first two. All of the apostle's various statements about Jesus' resurrection are expressions of faith. They proclaim faith's understanding of who Jesus was and continues to be: the One in whom God is definitively revealed and through whom God's saving purposes are fulfilled. They affirm that in the apparent weakness of the cross God's power was and continues to be present to give life. In short, the apostle conceives of Jesus' resurrection as an integral part of the one decisive saving event. As we have seen, he pays no special attention to "what happened" on Easter. His attention is focused, rather, on what the continuing presence of Jesus as the risen Lord means for humankind, and in particular for those who believe in the gospel.

The Risen Lord and the Resurrection Life

For Paul, the power of God that is evident in Jesus' resurrection is the same saving power that is present in Jesus' death. This is certainly the presupposition of statements like the one in Rom 4:25, that Christ "was handed over to death for our trespasses and was raised for our justification." Similarly, through the power of Christ's death and resurrection believers are able to "walk in newness of life" (Rom 6:4) and to "bear fruit for God" (Rom 7:4). And the apostle has the crucified-risen Lord in mind when he writes that "it is Christ who lives in me" (Gal 2:20). This is Paul's distinctive way of describing the powerful reality and continuing significance both of Jesus' death and of his resurrection.

However, experiencing the power of the crucified and risen Christ in one's life is not the same thing as being *resurrected with* Christ. (The Corinthian Christians evidently thought so, and in 1 Corinthians Paul is trying to straighten them out; see especially chapter 15.) Believers can only look forward to resurrection with Christ; it remains their hope (1 Cor 15:12–19; Phil 3:10–11). While God's saving power is even now at work, the fullness of salvation will come only in the future (Rom 5:9, 10; 8:18–25; 1 Thess 1:10). Not until then will one be united with Christ in his resurrection (Rom 6:5, 8). Meanwhile, one lives with hope, confident that "the one who raised the Lord Jesus will raise us also with Jesus, and will bring us ... into his presence" (2 Cor 4:14; compare 1 Cor 6:14; 1 Thess 4:14; 5:9–10). Christ is therefore described as the "first fruits" of the coming resurrection. His resurrection is the first part of the harvest that will be given in its fullness at the last day (1 Cor 15:20, 23).

Jesus Who is to Come

Jesus' expected return at the close of history is not as prominent a theme in Paul's letters as Jesus' death and resurrection. One could hardly imagine Paul saying, "I decided to know nothing among you except Jesus Christ, the one who is to come." Yet Paul expected Christ's return, and he expected it within his own lifetime (1 Thess 4:17; 1 Cor 15:51; compare 1 Cor 7:26, 29, 31; Phil 4:5; Rom 13:11–12). This is by no means an unimportant theme, and was certainly part of his missionary preaching (1 Thess 1:9–10).

The apostle never uses the phrase "second coming." One term that he does use is *parousia*, ordinarily translated into English as "coming" (1 Cor 15:23; 1 Thess 2:19; 3:13; 4:15; 5:23), though it can also mean "arrival" or "presence." More frequently, Paul refers to the coming "day" (Rom 2:5, 16; 13:12; 1 Cor 3:13), usually adding some kind of specific reference to Christ (1 Cor 1:8; 5:5; 2 Cor 1:14; Phil 1:6, 10; 2:26; 1 Thess 5:2). He can also write simply of "the end" (see especially, 1 Cor 15:24) – meaning not that "everything is over," but that God's power has prevailed and God's purposes have been fulfilled.

Paul's expectations concerning the close of history were shaped to a large extent by the views of the church before him. The earliest church, in turn, had been influenced in its thinking both by Jesus' preaching about the coming Reign of God, and by certain Jewish expectations about the last days. Thus, many of the apostle's statements about Christ's return make use of traditional Christian and Jewish concepts.

Two Scenarios: 1 Thessalonians 4:16–17; 1 Corinthians 15:12–28

Paul shows little concern for spelling out what exactly will happen when Christ comes again. Only in 1 Thessalonians and 1 Corinthians does he offer anything like a specific scenario, and in each case it is to help him make a special point.

In 1 Thess 4:13–18 he is assuring his congregation that believers who have died before the Lord's return will still be saved. It is to establish this that Paul describes a three-part event (vv. 16–17). First, "with a cry of command, with the archangel's call and with the sound of God's trumpet," the Lord "will descend from heaven." Second, those who have died "in Christ" will be resurrected. Third, with that accomplished, both they and those who are still alive will be "caught up in the clouds ... to meet the Lord in the air." The command, the archangel's call, the trumpet, the resurrection of the dead, and the clouds are all traditional elements of Jewish and Christian end-time scenarios. Paul is of course emphasizing the resurrection of those who have died, and that they will share in the "rapture" (being snatched up) to heaven. But also – and this is his special and climactic point – all of those who are thus enraptured will forever "be with the Lord."

The topic in 1 Corinthians 15 is also the resurrection of the dead. The major points in Paul's argument run approximately as follows. (1) Christ's own resurrection stands as the "first fruits" of the coming resurrection of those who belong to him (vv. 20, 23). (2) Should it be correct – as some Corinthians are saying – that there will be no resurrection of the dead, then Christ himself has not been raised (vv. 12–13, 15–16). (3) If Christ has not been raised, then Paul's gospel is invalid, and so is the faith of those in Corinth who have been converted by it (vv. 14, 17). (4) In addition, if Christ has not been raised from the dead, then there is no hope for those believers who have themselves died (vv. 18–19). (5) But since Christ has indeed been raised (vv. 4–8, 20), the coming resurrection of the dead is assured (vv. 21–23).

After emphasizing that the resurrection of the dead will occur upon Christ's return (vv. 21–23), the apostle pauses to portray the scene (vv. 24–28). Here, in contrast to 1 Thessalonians, he focuses on Christ's role in destroying every power that is opposed to God – including, finally, death itself (vv. 24–26). This is the one place in Paul's own letters where Christ is presented in the role of a king (v. 25). But that role will be temporary, we are told, because the kingdom is really God's. Thus, when death has been destroyed, Christ will deliver the kingdom to his Father and Christ himself will be subjected to God (vv. 24, 28).

Christ, the Final Judgment, and the Final Glory

Paul does not describe a final judgment in either one of his end-time scenarios. There is no doubt that he expected a final judgment, however, and that he envisioned a role in that for Christ. In some places he identifies the Judge as Christ, while in other places he thinks of God himself in that role (contrast 2 Cor 5:10 [Christ] with Rom 14:10 [God]). His more considered view is perhaps the one in Rom 2:16 – that at the end, "God, *through* Jesus Christ, will judge the secret thoughts of all."

The apostle is confident that for those who have remained faithful to the gospel the coming day of the Lord will be a day of "salvation," not of "wrath" (1 Thess 1:10; 5:9; 1 Cor 5:5). But "salvation" is not the only term he uses to describe what is in store for the faithful. Among his various other expressions for what awaits them are: "the kingdom" (1 Thess 2:12), "justification" (Rom 5:16), resurrection with Christ (Rom 6:5, 8), "eternal life" (Rom 6:22–23), "glory" (Rom 2:7).

Paul's expectation that believers will come to share in the glory of God is especially important. It is closely related to his understanding of Jesus as a kind of "second Adam." Although the first Adam (representing humanity as a whole) had been crowned with "glory and honor" at creation (see Ps 8:4, 5), he destroyed that glory by his disobedience (Rom 3:23; 5:12–21). But in Christ, according to Paul, the glory has been restored (see especially, 1 Cor 15:42–49). Thus, Paul can think of those who are in Christ as "being transformed" already into Christ's image, "from one degree of glory to another" (2 Cor 3:18). Yet the fulfillment of this process, the total "revealing" of this glory, remains a hope (Rom 5:2; 8:14–24; 2 Cor 4:17; Phil 3:21). Only at the Lord's return, following the resurrection of the dead, will it be complete.

The apostle has relatively little to say about what it will mean to experience the coming "glory." According to 1 Corinthians 15, being "raised in glory" will mean being raised with a "spiritual" body as distinct from a "physical" one (vv. 43–44). What is "perishable" will be replaced with what is "imperishable" (v. 42). What is "of the dust" will be replaced with what is "of heaven" (vv. 47–49). This is the "change" of which Paul writes in vv. 51–53, the "victory" which he is confident that God will achieve through Christ at his return (vv. 54–57).

The hope expressed in Romans 8 is similar. Here the apostle

writes of "the glory about to be revealed to us," equating it with "the revealing of the children of God" (vv. 18–19). He is thinking specifically of "the *freedom* of the glory of the children of God," including "the redemption of our bodies" (vv. 21, 23). He means freedom from both sin and death, and declares that even the whole of creation "will be set free from its bondage to decay" (v. 21).

Paul's reference here to "the revealing *of the children of God*" is significant. To be "glorified" will not mean some kind of "absorption" into God's being. Freedom from death and decay will not mean being set free from God. Rather, "sharing the glory of God" (Rom 5:2) will mean the freedom fully to *be* God's children, to know and to be present for God, just as God has always known and been present for them. It is this about which Paul expressed his confidence in 2 Cor 4:14 – that after being raised with Christ, believers will be brought into the presence of God (see also 1 Thess 4:17). Similarly, 1 Cor 13:12: "*then* we will see face to face ... *then* I will know fully, even as I have been fully known."

Jesus and the Community of Faith

One sometimes hears Jesus described as a "personal Savior." Insofar as this suggests that believers can have a personally meaningful relationship with him as their Lord, the description is true to Paul's own experience. But insofar as it may suggest that believers can enjoy a *private* relationship with Jesus, it runs directly counter to Paul's gospel. He of course does not deny the validity of what might be called a private religious life. Proper to that category, as he sees it, are such manifestations of the Spirit as speaking in tongues (1 Cor 14:2, 4a) and other ecstatic experiences (2 Cor 5:13a). But where he finds Jesus most significantly present is not in the private experiences of individual believers. It is within the believing *community*. Where people share in the "body" of Christ, are committed to fulfilling the "law" of Christ, and bear faithful witness to the gospel of Christ, there, according to Paul, Jesus' presence is truly experienced.

Sharing in the Body of Christ

The apostle's most extensive comments about the believing community as Christ's "body" are in 1 Cor 12:12–28. It is important to observe that, for Paul, Christ is not himself one of the members of this body. (The notion of Christ as the body's "head" appears first in the literature of the "Pauline school," discussed in chapter 5.) Christ *is* the body, it is he who gives the body its identity. Thus, the body of Christ is more than the sum of its individual members.

The nature of Christian community is also apparent when Paul refers to it as a *koinonia*. This word is often translated "fellowship," as in 1 Cor 1:9: "God is faithful; by him you were called into the fellowship of his Son, Jesus Christ our Lord." That is too weak a translation, however, since in our everyday speech "fellowship" often means simply "enjoying one another's company." But Paul is referring to something more like a "partnership," as when business partners hold shares in a reality which transcends even their pooled resources. (The Greek word *koinonia* was in fact used for such corporate entities.) According to Paul, the call into Christ's *koinonia* is a summons to be in-corporate with him, and thus to participate in the corporate reality of the community of faith.

In 1 Corinthians 12 Paul writes about the unity of the body into which believers have been incorporated. But he stresses even more the diversity of the spiritual gifts with which its members have been graced, and their consequent need for one another. In this connection he singles out the weak and the needy for special mention. The weaker members are "indispensable" for the body's proper functioning, he says (v. 22), and God is particularly concerned for the needy (v. 24 – where NRSV's translation, "the inferior member," should be corrected to "the needy member"). For this reason, members are called to "care for one another," and to rejoice and suffer as one (vv. 25–26).

Paul's comments about sharing in suffering need to be placed in the context of his whole gospel. He understands the gospel, we recall, as the strange, saving power of God's love as that has been disclosed in the cross. Accordingly, he interprets his own apostolic sufferings as "carrying in the body the death of Jesus" (2 Cor 4:10). They are a vital part of his apostolic ministry. Moreover, he suggests that these very same sufferings are manifested within the believing community (2 Cor 1:6–7). Believers are thereby sharing Christ's sufferings and being conformed to his death (Rom 8:17; Phil 3:10). Just as baptism into the body of Christ (1 Cor 12:13; Gal 3:27) signals baptism into Christ's death (Rom 6:3–4), so sharing in the body of Christ means, in part, sharing in Christ's sufferings. Paul has in view not only sufferings that may be brought about by "enemies of the cross of Christ" (Phil 3:18), as in Phil 1:27–30. He is also thinking of those who, like Christ himself, risk their own welfare by giving themselves to the service of the weak and the needy (Rom 15:1–3).

Fulfilling the Law of Christ

In Paul's day there was no understanding of the role of the human circulatory system in nourishing and enlivening the body. If there had been, we can imagine that he might have extended his image of the body of Christ to take that into account. In doing so, he surely would have identified love as the life-force that circulates within the believing community to sustain and energize it. He would have meant, first, God's love as disclosed in Christ, and then also God's love as it comes to be manifested in the lives of the members of the body.

In Rom 13:9 and Gal 5:13 the apostle declares that all of the law's commandments are summed up in the one commandment to love the neighbor as oneself (Lev 19:18); thus it is love that fulfills the law (Rom 13:8, 10). This must be what Paul means when he writes about "the law of Christ" (Gal 6:2; 1 Cor 9:21). He is not thinking of some collection of Jesus' teachings, as if those constitute a new "Christian law" that has replaced the old law of Moses. He could, just possibly, be thinking specifically of what Jesus taught about love, including the commandment to bless, not curse, one's persecutors (see above, pp. 53–55). But more probably, or at least more significantly, he is thinking of Jesus' death. For Paul, what constitutes "the law of Christ" is the love which faith sees in the cross, and which, in seeing, it trusts and obeys.

Both of Paul's references to Christ's "law" occur in contexts where he is expressing concern for those who need the special care of other members of the body. In Galatians 6 those are the brothers and sisters who have committed some specific transgression (v. 1). Concerning them Paul counsels: "Bear one another's burdens, and in this way you will fulfill the law of Christ" (v. 2). In 1 Corinthians 8–10 he is thinking of the "weak" in conscience, who continue to have scruples about eating meat that has been slaughtered in pagan rites (8:7–13). In this case he urges that the stronger identify with the weaker (note 9:22), remembering that Christ died also for them (8:11), and realizing that to wound their conscience would be to sin against Christ himself (8:12).

Since God's love is the life of the body of Christ, when love does not circulate among its members Christ's body is profaned. This is exactly the point of Paul's warnings about the disorders which are occurring during observances of the Lord's Supper in Corinth (1 Cor 11:17–34). Those should be celebrations of the community's partnership in Christ (1 Cor 10:16–17). Instead, they have become occasions for division, when the better-off members of the congregation humiliate those who "have nothing" (1 Cor 11:17–22). By thus dishonoring one another they are dishonoring the body of Christ (11:27–29), and failing to proclaim the Lord's death until he comes (11:26).

Bearing Witness to the Gospel of Christ

So far we have considered only Paul's views about Jesus' continuing presence within the community of faith. What he has to say about this, however, must not be isolated from what he suggests about Jesus' presence for "the world." According to Paul, those who have come to know Jesus as the Christ are thereby called to bear witness to his gospel where it has not yet been heard. In and through their witness, Jesus becomes present as well for others.

In his own case, Paul feels the special urgency of bearing this witness: "Woe to me if I do not proclaim the gospel" (1 Cor 9:16; compare 1:17). He is devoted to taking the gospel where Christ has not yet been named (Rom 15:20; 2 Cor 10:15–16). He likens his mission to that of a political emissary. The apostles, he says, are "ambassadors for Christ" (2 Cor 5:20). That is, through their presence and witness, Christ himself is given a presence in a new place.

Paul by no means restricts this task to specially designated persons, like apostles. The faith community as a whole, and each of its members, is also called to bear witness to the gospel of Christ. While Paul insists that membership in Christ's body gives believers a distinctive identity within the world, he does not mean that they should live a sectarian existence apart from the world (1 Cor 5:9–10). On the contrary, believers are counseled to "remain" in the social location where they were when they responded to the gospel (1 Cor 7:17–24). Only now, of course, they are there as persons who are "with God," and who belong to the Lord (1 Cor 7:22–24). This is in fact their witness, according to Paul. As "children of God without blemish in the midst of a crooked and perverse generation," they are to "shine like stars in the world" (Phil 2:15).

Summary

If we could ask Paul what it means to "know Jesus," he would not answer in terms of knowing certain facts about Jesus' earthly life and ministry. Rather, we could expect him to answer along the lines of his own faith statement in Philippians 3. When he writes there about "knowing Christ Jesus my Lord" (v. 8), he is referring to his present and ongoing relationship to Jesus as a living presence. He is thinking of being "in" Christ (v. 9), of belonging to him (v. 14), of sharing his sufferings, his death, and – ultimately – the power of his resurrection (vv. 10–11). This is not just "fact knowledge" but "faith knowledge." It is, moreover, the kind of knowledge that finds expression always within a *community* of believers – where women and men of faith know Jesus as the Christ by sharing in his "body," fulfilling his "law," and bearing witness to his gospel.

Chapter 5

Jesus According to the "Pauline School"

Introduction

Everything that has been said so far about Paul's understanding of Jesus has been based on an examination of the seven letters which virtually all scholars regard as unquestionably authentic: Romans, 1 and 2 Corinthians, Galatians, Philippians, 1 Thessalonians, and Philemon. Now in this chapter we must consider the six other New Testament writings which bear Paul's name, but whose actual authorship is in doubt: Ephesians, Colossians, 2 Thessalonians, 1 and 2 Timothy, and Titus. The view adopted here, in agreement with many other scholars, is that all six of these were written after Paul's death. It is probable that 1 and 2 Timothy and Titus, the so-called "Pastoral Epistles," were written by the same person. Three separate authors seem to have been responsible for Ephesians, Colossians, and 2 Thessalonians. In no case, however, can the real author be identified.

The Question of Authorship

Several different factors have a bearing on the question of authorship. First there is the matter of *style and vocabulary*. The style of a person's writing – grammar, sentence structure, and so forth – is almost like a signature, distinctive and relatively consistent. In various ways, the six questionable letters depart from Pauline style. In addition, they sometimes use words not found in the unquestionably authentic letters; and, more important, they sometimes use Pauline words in quite non-Pauline ways.

Second, scholars have been led to question the authenticity of these letters because of the various *anachronisms* they contain or involve. That is, they often presuppose certain events or situations which do not square with what we know to have been the case during Paul's lifetime. There is, for example, the way Paul himself is presented. Especially from Ephesians, Colossians, and the Pastoral Epistles, one receives the impression that Paul was an apostle without equal and of unquestioned authority. There is not a word about Peter or the "pillar apostles" of Jerusalem (contrast Galatians), and Paul's conduct and preaching seem to be quite unchallenged (contrast 1 and 2 Corinthians, as well as Galatians). Another example, from 2 Thess 2:1–2, is the mention of certain erroneous teachings which have been circulated in a letter falsely claiming to be from Paul. During the apostle's own lifetime, however, his opponents would have had no need to resort to this kind of deceit. On the evidence of the unquestionably authentic letters, we know that Paul's critics were quite open and direct in opposing his views with their own.

Third, each of these six letters represents a *point of view* which is to some extent different from Paul's views, as known from the seven undisputed letters. This is the case precisely, and especially, when these later writers refer to Jesus. The "cross" is mentioned only in Eph 2:16; Col 1:20; 2:14, and references to Christ's resurrection and exaltation sometimes overshadow references to his death. There is no sense here that Jesus will return any time soon – and in Ephesians, there is no mention at all of his expected return. While familiar Pauline themes are echoed at various points, at least as many of the statements about Jesus' significance have been drawn from or influenced by general churchly traditions.

The "Pauline School"

Ephesians, Colossians, 2 Thessalonians, and the Pastoral Epistles are usually described as "deutero-Pauline" by those who regard them as inauthentic. The letters are thus judged to have a "secondary" status – the designation "deutero" is from the Greek word *deuteros*, which means "second." They are "secondary-Paul" because they show how he was being interpreted in the church after his death, and not necessarily what he had actually taught and done. However, it would be quite wrong to think of those who produced the deutero-Pauline writings as "forgers." They were not out for personal gain. Rather, they were concerned to address the needs of the church in their day – roughly, the period from 65 through 125 – by invoking the name and authority of Paul, the late and now revered martyr-apostle.

In this connection, some New Testament scholars have chosen to speak about a "Pauline school." It is well known that various other teachers of Paul's day (for example, the Hellenistic moral philosophers, Musonius Rufus and Epictetus) established academies which continued on after their deaths. In these continuing schools, the founders' teachings and writings were interpreted, adapted, applied, and even supplemented. There is no clear evidence that Paul had ever established such an academy, or even that his associates established one after his death. Nonetheless, the apostle's teachings and ministry continued to be a subject of discussion and debate within the congregations that he had established. So at least in this sense, Paul's congregations functioned rather like "schools." There his letters continued to be interpreted, adapted, applied, and supplemented.

The two largest and most important centers of Pauline activity had been Ephesus in Asia Minor and Corinth in Greece. In these cities, particularly, one can imagine that there would have been both the interest and the resources to assemble, preserve, and interpret Paul's letters. It may have been in one or both of these cities, as well, that the various deutero-Pauline writings were produced.

The four deutero-Pauline writers hold certain fundamental convictions and points of view in common. First, they all regard Paul's letters as normative, and Paul himself as the prime guarantor of the true apostolic tradition. Second, they are all more interested in Paul himself, as an example of Christian faith and endurance, than they are in Paul's thought. Third, they all seem to presuppose an indefinite interval before the Lord's return, and therefore an indefinitely extended need for the church and individual believers to come to terms with the present world. A final point follows from the first three. These writers are all less concerned to think new thoughts and create new traditions than they are to interpret, stabilize, and defend the old ones. They are not trying to be original. They are trying to be faithful spokespersons for Paul's gospel – as they understand that – even while facing issues, both practical and theological, that the apostle himself did not have to face.

We should not suppose, however, that anything like a uniform "deutero-Pauline theology" can be identified. Each of these writers has a somewhat distinctive set of issues to address, and they approach those in their own distinctive ways. This will become apparent as we consider how each of them views the status and role of Jesus.

Colossians

Colossians was perhaps the first of the deutero-Paulines produced. It could have been written as early as the year 65, but hardly later than the year 90. A more precise dating is impossible. The church in Colossae, a city of Asia Minor, had been founded by a certain Epaphras (Col 1:7). Paul himself seems never to have visited there (Col 2:1). Colossae was devastated by an earthquake in 60–61 and not rebuilt until the second century. Thus, if Colossians is indeed a deutero-Pauline letter, the intended recipients must have been living elsewhere. One good possibility is that they were in neighboring Laodicea (see Col 4:13–16), which had been quickly rebuilt after the earthquake.

The Situation Addressed

Whoever the intended recipients of this letter, it is apparent that the writer is concerned to combat certain false teachings to which they have been attracted (see especially, 2:8–23).

At the root of these teachings was some notion about various cosmic powers which were thought to exercise control over people's lives (2:8, 15, 20). It was apparently believed that deliverance from those powers could only be achieved by abstaining from certain foods (and perhaps also from sex), by observing certain festival and holy days, and by special acts of worship (either of or along with angels).

Colossians is written to combat such ideas. The readers are encouraged to "continue steadfast in the faith" (1:23) – which means, specifically, in "Christ Jesus the Lord" (2:6–7). This writer's basic affirmation is that faith in Christ is sufficient for salvation, including deliverance from whatever cosmic powers there be. For this reason, the concern in Colossians is quite specifically christological. That is, Christ and his saving significance stand at the very center of this author's message.

Colossians 1:15–20

In a prominent place near the beginning of this letter the author has included a hymn in praise of Christ (1:15–20). To this he has probably made at least two significant additions.

The christological affirmations of this hymn are fundamental to everything else in Colossians. It may be divided into two parts, each with its own particular emphasis.

The first part of the hymn (vv. 15–18a) affirms Christ's role in and therefore supremacy over all creation. He is identified closely with God ("the image of the invisible God") and is described as "the firstborn of all creation" (v. 15). By this it is meant not only that "all things have been created through him," but also that all things have been created "*for* him" (v. 16). Thus, in the statement that "He himself is before all things" (v. 17), the word "before" makes two points about Christ's status. It affirms that Christ precedes all things in time, and also that he is pre-eminent over all things. The latter point is emphasized in the last line of this first part of the hymn: "He is the head of the body" (v. 18a). The identification of "the body" with the church is probably an addition from the author of Colossians. But in the hymn itself the "body" designates the whole cosmic order. Christ's sovereignty is thus portrayed as absolute and universal – an idea with which our author surely agrees, despite his specific reference to the church (see, for example, 2:10). Since Christ is sovereign it follows that "in him all things hold together" (v. 17). The whole cosmos is understood to be sustained and unified by Christ's power.

The second part of the hymn (vv. 18b–20) affirms Christ's role in and supremacy over the *new* creation. Thus, when he is called "the beginning," that is explained with reference to his being "the firstborn of the dead" (v. 18b). Christ's resurrection anticipates and assures the resurrection that is yet to come. Moreover, as the one in whom "all the fullness of God was pleased to dwell" (v. 19) he is also the agent of God's reconciling work: "through him God was pleased to reconcile to himself all things, whether on earth or in heaven, by making peace ... " (v. 20).

The comment that reconciliation was accomplished "through the blood of his cross" (v. 20) is probably another addition to the hymn by the author of Colossians. The idea, though not the wording, is thoroughly Pauline (Rom 5:6–11; 2 Cor 5:14–19), and it is echoed also in Col 1:22 and 2:14. But the focus of the hymn itself is on the cosmic Christ, transcendent over history. It is not on Christ's appearance within history, and certainly not on the weakness of the cross.

The Mystery of Christ

The author of Colossians uses various phrases to describe Paul's gospel, including "the word of the truth" (1:5), "the word of God" (1:25), and "the mystery of Christ" (4:3). The latter is especially appropriate, given the message that this author is concerned to get across to his readers. He wants them to understand that Christ himself is "God's mystery," because in Christ "are hidden all the treasures of wisdom and knowledge" (2:2–3). That is, in Christ faith sees and receives all that is necessary for salvation. Christ is above all, and all-sufficient.

These statements about Christ are intended to counter the false teachings to which the readers are being attracted. The point is being made that commitment to Christ neither requires nor allows the espousal of additional religious doctrines and practices. Those "are only a shadow of what is to come," while "the substance belongs to Christ" (2:17). There is no greater wisdom, no deeper mystery than "the riches of assured understanding" (2:2) which are disclosed in Christ. The writer's basic appeal follows from this (2:6–7):

[6]As you therefore have received Christ Jesus the Lord, continue to live your lives in him, [7]rooted and built up in him and established in the faith, just as you were taught, abounding in thanksgiving.

Resurrection with Christ

Picking up one of the hymnic affirmations of 1:15–20, this author emphasizes that Christ is the sovereign "head of every ruler and authority" (2:10; compare 1:16, 18a). He also draws from the hymn the point that one can discern in Christ "the whole fullness of deity" (2:9; compare 1:19). In affirming this, however, our anonymous writer makes two significant additions. First, he specifies that in Christ "the whole fullness of deity dwells *bodily*" (2:9). The hymn itself, as we have noted, does not have the incarnate life of Jesus in view. For this writer, though, the historical dimension of Christ's lordship is important (see also 1:22). Second, he goes on to refer to believers as having "come to fullness" in Christ (2:10). To be sure, the hymn declares that in Christ "God was pleased to reconcile to himself all things" (1:20). But the author of Colossians goes far beyond that in describing the significance of this reconciliation for the community of faith.

The "fullness" which believers experience in Christ is described in 2:11–15. Baptism (called a "spiritual circumcision," v. 11) is said to represent, in part, burial with Christ (v. 12), hence the "putting off" of old ways (vv. 11, 13–14a). Therefore, as in 1:20b, 22, Jesus' death is identified as the saving event. Here a particularly striking metaphor is employed to describe divine forgiveness: God "set aside" the certificate of moral indebtedness, "nailing it to the cross" (2:14b).

Both of these points, the saving significance of Jesus' death, and baptism as symbolic of burial with Christ, are recognizably Pauline (Rom 5:6–8; 6:3–11). However, the author of Colossians departs from Paul when he writes of baptism as symbolic also of *resurrection* with Christ (2:12):

when you were buried with him in baptism, you were also raised with him through faith in the power of God, who raised him from the dead.

For Paul himself, the saving power of the cross is already evident in a new way of life (Rom 6:4). But the apostle does not describe that as resurrection with Christ. For Paul himself, resurrection with Christ remains a hope (Rom 6:5, 8). It is otherwise for the author of Colossians. Here, for example, the appeal to lead a new life is based on the presupposition that believers have already been resurrected with Christ: "Since you have been raised with Christ, seek the things that are above, where Christ is, seated at the right hand of God (Col 3:1; NRSV, modified).

Concluding Observations

In Colossians we are introduced to a cosmic Christ, one who transcends all time and space. The incarnation is not lost sight of, nor the saving significance of Christ's death upon the cross. However, neither Jesus' earthly life nor his teachings come into view. The emphasis remains on Christ's timeless, sovereign rule. Here the central christological image is not of Christ hanging on a cross, but of Christ enthroned at the right hand of God. Indeed, for this writer Paul's vision of Christ's final victory over every cosmic power (1 Cor 15:23, 24–28) has already been realized (Col 2:10, 15). Thus, believers have already been "transferred ... into the kingdom of [God's] beloved Son" (1:13). This writer does not, however, share the view of Paul's Corinthian opponents that Christian hope has been completely fulfilled in the present life of faith. For him, as for Paul, with Christ's indwelling presence is given "the hope of glory" (1:28), and that will be fulfilled only at Christ's return (3:4).

Ephesians

There are striking similarities between Colossians and Ephesians, not only in the ideas they contain but also in the way certain statements are worded (compare, for example, Col 1:20–22 and Eph 2:13–18; Col 2:19 and Eph 4:16; Col 4:7–8 and Eph 6:21–22). The most plausible explanation is that the author of Ephesians has made use of Colossians. Ephesians is thus to be dated later than Colossians, but probably no later than about the year 95.

Although Ephesians exhibits certain formal characteristics of the usual Pauline letter, it reads more like a sermon or essay. Unlike Colossians, for example, no specific congregational situation seems to be in view. In fact, the phrase "in Ephesus" (1:1) may well be a later addition to the address (see NRSV footnote). Apart from those two words, there is nothing which requires us to conclude that this letter was composed specifically for the Ephesian church. The author's concern is not with particular local problems, but for the faith and life of Christians in general. That he has Gentile Christians in mind is certain; and it is likely that his letter was first circulated in Asia Minor. Beyond these points, however, we know nothing about its intended destination.

Christ and the Church

This author's main interests are clearly evident in the opening blessing (1:3–14) and thanksgiving (1:15–23). He is concerned that his readers understand "the mystery of [God's] will" as that has been "set forth in Christ" (1:9). God's will is described as "a plan for the fullness of time," to unite all things in Christ (1:10). This plan is said to be accomplished through the power by which Christ has been raised from the dead and enthroned as sovereign over all other rulers, whether of this age or of the next (1:20–21). For this writer it is especially important that Christ has been made "the head over all things *for the church*," which is described as "his body" and "the fullness of him who fills all in all" (1:22–23). Or, changing the metaphor, he can portray Christ as the "cornerstone" of the church. In him the whole building not only "holds together" but actually "grows into a holy temple in the Lord" (2:20–22).

Here and throughout Ephesians the cosmic christology of Colossians is being presupposed. It is, indeed, foundational for all of this author's other affirmations and appeals. Yet the main topic in Ephesians is not Christ but the church. This author conceives of the church, just as he conceives of Christ, in cosmic terms. It transcends both space and time. It is "through the church" that the riches of God's wisdom are "made known to the rulers and authorities in the heavenly places" (3:10). And not only "in Christ Jesus," but also "in the church," God is glorified "to all generations, forever and ever" (3:21).

It is first of all this cosmic status of the church of which the author is thinking in 2:11–18. As "the fullness" of Christ (1:23), in whom all things have been gathered together (1:10), the church is a vital part of God's plan for cosmic unity. Specifically, in the church those who were once "far off" from God "have been brought near" to him (2:13, 18). The church is thus constituent of the "one new humanity" which comes into being when "the law with its commandments and ordinances" is abolished (2:14–16). Where there was once alienation, division, and hostility there is now unity. The author describes this unity as "peace," which he identifies with Christ (2:14, 17) and attributes to Christ's death on the cross (2:15–16).

The unity and peace of this "one new humanity" also come into view in 4:1–6, where the author introduces a long series of ethical appeals (4:7–6:20). Believers are urged to conduct themselves in accord with their calling, "bearing with one another in love" and "making every effort to maintain the unity of the Spirit in the bond of peace" (4:1–3). For they belong to "one body and one Spirit," they share "one hope," and they know "one Lord, one faith, one baptism, one God and Father of all, who is above all and through all and in all" (4:4–6).

It is thus apparent that what the author of Ephesians has to say about Christ cannot be separated from what he says about the church. His two key affirmations about Christ are also two of his key affirmations about the church: Christ is "the head" of the body, which is the church; and the church is "the fullness" of Christ (1:22–23). Each of these points deserves further comment.

Christ the Head of the Church

To affirm that Christ is the head of the church is to affirm both his authority over it and that he is the source of its life and strength. This idea has been taken over from Colossians, not from the letters of Paul. The apostle himself had not identified Christ with the "head" of the body, but with the body as such. As we have seen, the original Pauline conception is that the members of the body are jointly incorporated into Christ (see above, pp. 88–89). In 1 Corinthians 12 Paul mentions the head as simply one of those members, no less or more important than any other (v. 21). And in Romans 12 he writes of the Christian community as "one body *in* Christ" (v. 5), not – as he might have – of "one body, with Christ as its head." Thus, when the author of Colossians, quoting a hymn which describes Christ as "the head of the body," proceeds to identify that body as "the church" (1:18), the Pauline metaphor has been significantly altered. The image resurfaces in Col 2:19, where it is suggested that the body grows only insofar as its members hold fast to Christ the head. The author's point is that those who depart from the gospel of Christ divide and diminish the church.

This image of Christ's headship is developed further and in other directions in Ephesians. First, in 4:15–16 the point of Col 2:19 is given a specifically moral application. It is by "speaking the truth in love" that the members of the body will "grow up in every way into him who is the head, into Christ" (v. 15). The body's "growth" is thereby understood to be growth in love (v. 16). Then in Eph 5:21–6:9 Christ's authority over the church is offered as the model for relationships within the Christian household. (This is not the case in the parallel passage, Col 3:18–4:1.) The author's introductory statement (5:21) expresses his view of the principle which is to govern every domestic relationship: "Be subject to one another out of reverence for Christ." Subsequently, wives are told to be subject to their husbands (5:22–24), children are told to obey their parents (6:1–3), and slaves are told to obey their masters (6:5–8). This is in line with the cultural norms of that day, according to which women, children, and slaves were to remain subordinate to those regarded as their superiors.

The more distinctively Christian admonitions are the ones addressed, respectively, to husbands, parents, and masters. Husbands are told to love their wives (5:25–33), parents are told not to provoke their children (6:4), and masters are told not to threaten their slaves (6:9). These appeals transform an otherwise traditional, patriarchal domestic code into one that reflects what some interpreters have called a "love patriarchalism." The model offered for this is Christ's relationship to the church. That relationship is spelled out only in the instructions directed to husbands and wives, but it is doubtless presumed in the other cases as well.

Above all, Christ is regarded as the church's "Savior" (5:23), in that he "loved the church and gave himself up for her" (5:25; compare v. 29). This interpretation of Christ's death as an act of selfless, saving love is also evident in 5:2, and it is thoroughly Pauline. However, the view that the saving benefits of Christ's death are bestowed through baptism (5:26) cannot be found in Paul's letters (contrast Rom 6:3–4). Nor had the apostle ever referred to the church *itself* as destined to be presented, finally, to God as "holy and without blemish"

(5:27). This lofty vision of the church is explained by the author's view that Christ is its "fullness" as well as its head.

Christ the Fullness of the Church

Here we encounter another affirmation about Christ which develops an idea that the writer has found in Colossians. According to the author of Colossians, "the whole fullness of deity dwells bodily" in Christ (2:9), and believers "have come to fullness in him," who rules as head over the cosmos (2:10). In the first instance the term "fullness" identifies Christ as God incarnate (compare 1:19). In the second instance it points to the new life which is given to those who have been buried and resurrected with Christ (note 2:11–14).

In Ephesians, too, there are references to the fullness of God and of Christ. The goal of the Christian life is said to be "the unity of the faith and of the knowledge of the Son of God" (4:13a). This is then described as gaining "maturity" and experiencing "the fullness of Christ" (4:13b; NRSV, modified). Given the comments in 3:19, knowing God's Son and experiencing his fullness would seem to mean experiencing "the love of Christ," whereby one is "filled with all the fullness of God." One hears in these two passages unmistakable echoes of Col 1:19 and 2:9, 10.

In a third reference to the fullness of Christ (Eph 4:10), our author declares that Christ has been exalted "far above all the heavens" in order that he might "fill all things" (that is, the whole cosmos). There is at least an intimation of this idea in Colossians (3:11; compare 1:16–18, 20). A comparison with Paul's thought, however, will bring out its distinctiveness. According to the apostle (1 Cor 15:24–28), at the close of history Christ will hand over the kingdom to his Father (vv. 24–26). Then Christ himself will be subjected to his Father, "so that God may be all in all" (v. 28). Here in Ephesians one notes two important differences. Paul's comment about God has been applied to Christ, and Christ's filling of the whole cosmos is presumed to be a present reality. For this reason the author does not hesitate to refer to the kingdom as belonging to Christ as well as to God (5:5).

Finally, according to Ephesians Christ's cosmic presence is uniquely exhibited in the church, "the fullness of him who fills all in all" (1:23). This is in keeping with, but says more than the comments about believers experiencing "the fullness of Christ" (3:19; 4:13). The point is not that Christ is present only in the church but that he is perfectly present there. His sovereignty over the church is unrivalled, therefore unlimited. Here as elsewhere in Ephesians the church is viewed as a cosmic entity, and therefore as a vital part of God's plan for salvation.

Concluding Observations

The christology of Ephesians has been influenced both by Paul's letters and by Colossians. Part of this author's Pauline legacy is his view of Christ's death as an act of saving, reconciling love (1:7; 2:13–18; 5:2, 25–27). Related to this, and distinctive to his own presentation, is his description of Christ as "our peace" (2:14–15; compare 2:17; 4:3; 6:15). His thought is of Christ's role as mediator between heaven and earth, the one who provides access to God (2:18; 3:11–12).

From Colossians the writer has drawn his perception of Christ as cosmic Lord, enthroned with God high above every other power in heaven and on earth (1:9–10, 20–23; 2:6; 4:9–10). He also shares the view that believers have already been raised up with Christ (2:4–5) – yes, even enthroned with him in heaven (2:6; compare 1:3).

What distinguishes the christology in Ephesians is the way Christ's status and role have been defined in relation to the church. Christ is its cornerstone, its head, its fullness, its Savior. Thus, without Christ the church cannot exist. In their own ways both Paul and the author of Colossians say the same. But the author of Ephesians says more: Christ cannot do without the church, either. As it is presented in Ephesians, the church, along with Christ, is an indispensable part of God's plan for salvation. As the domain where Christ's fullness is perfectly present (1:23), the church is also the agency through which God's wisdom is revealed to every cosmic power (3:10), and the place where God himself is glorified (3:21).

Second Thessalonians

It is evident that the author of 2 Thessalonians made use of 1 Thessalonians, but the parallels with Paul's letter are more superficial than those between Colossians and Ephesians (compare, for example, 1 Thess 1:1 and 2 Thess 1:1–2; 1 Thess 1:2–10 and 2 Thess 1:3–4; 1 Thess 5:23 and 2 Thess 3:16). While this writer, like Paul in 1 Thessalonians, has things to say about Christ's expected return (the *parousia*), we shall see that his point of view is significantly different from the apostle's. Where 2 Thessalonians was written, by whom, and for whom, can no longer be determined. As for the date, since the author wants his letter to be accepted as Paul's own (3:17) it is likely that some collection of the apostle's letters was already in circulation. If so, then it is likely that 2 Thessalonians was written sometime in the last decade of the first century.

The Purpose of the Letter

The author's purpose is clear. He is writing in order to correct the belief of some believers that the day of the Lord's return has in some sense already arrived (2:1–2). What may have prompted such an idea he does not say. He indicates only that those who believe this to be the case have claimed the support of Paul's own teaching (note 2:2).

Our author has to respond to this situation in two ways. First, he must counteract the authority of the letter which has been used to support the idea that he opposes. That letter, he claims, is not really Paul's (2:2), while the present letter really is (3:17). He wants his readers to accept *this* letter as containing the apostle's actual teaching about Christ's return.

Second, he must offer a plausible argument against the view that the *parousia* has already begun. In brief, his contention is that there are still many events that have to take place before the Lord returns. In the meantime believers are to remain faithful to the Pauline traditions (2:15) and to the example of the apostle's own life (3:6–13).

The Lord's Return

The author's main point is made succinctly in 2:3:

> Let no one deceive you in any way; for that day will not come unless the rebellion comes first and the lawless one is revealed, the one destined for destruction.

Whether "the lawless one" is to be identified with some heavenly figure or with some specific human being is unclear. By "the rebellion" the author doubtless means the period of apostasy and various attendant evils which, according to traditional apocalyptic expectations, would precede the close of history (see, for example, 2 Esdr 5:1–12). The readers are to understand that the time has not yet come for the Lord's return, since this final rebellion against God has not yet occurred.

In 2:1–10 the lawless one and his rebellion are described further. The scenario remains obscure in its details, especially the reference to something (or someone) which is restraining the lawless one until the time for his destruction (vv. 6–8). But again, the writer's message is clear: although the rebellion is already evident "in the working of Satan" (v. 9), until it has run its course the Lord cannot have returned.

What the Lord's return will actually be like is not as such the topic of 2 Thessalonians. Two points are clear, nonetheless. First, those who have remained faithful to the gospel, even when it has brought them persecution and affliction (1:4), will be rewarded. Their acceptance into "the kingdom of God" (1:5) will bring them relief from their suffering (1:7). It will also bring them into the Lord's own presence, where he will be "glorified" among them and they in him (1:9–10, 12; 2:14). Second, when the Lord returns he will wreak vengeance on those who have not obeyed the gospel, cutting them off forever from his presence and his glory (1:6, 8–9; 2:11–12). This will of course be the fate of the lawless one, too, "whom the Lord will destroy with the breath of his mouth ... " (2:3).

The Present Time

If the day of the Lord has not yet arrived, then what of the present? Our author has nothing specific to say about the present relationship of believers to Christ. For example – and in contrast with Paul and the authors of Colossians and Ephesians – he never refers to life "in Christ." (The reference in 1:12 to being glorified "in him" looks to the future; see 2:14). Rather, for this writer faith involves believing "the truth" (2:12, 13; compare v. 10), which the readers are to identify with what Paul has taught (1:10; 2:5, 14, 15; 3:6, 10) and now reiterates in this letter (3:14). And believing what Paul has taught means obeying it (1:8; 3:14).

Above all, obedience to Paul's teachings requires abandoning the mistaken notion that the day of the Lord has arrived. This is the point to which the first two chapters of the letter are devoted. But then in chapter 3 the author adds another appeal.

Obeying Paul's teachings also requires working for one's own living, as the apostle himself did (3:7–13). Is our author thinking of those who have given up their jobs because they believe that the day of the Lord has already come? Or is he simply expanding on the appeals that he has found in 1 Thess 4:11 and 5:14a? In either case, the readers are also advised to distance themselves from those who depend on others for their livelihood (3:6). The similar appeal in 3:14–15 is more general, and applies as well to anyone who has departed from Paul's teaching about the day of the Lord. All who refuse to accept the teachings of the present letter are to be avoided. The objective, apparently, is to shame them into changing their minds and their ways.

Concluding Observations

In 2 Thessalonians Christ is portrayed exclusively as the one who is to come. There is not a word here about Jesus' earthly life, his teachings, his death, or his resurrection; and not a word, either, about his enthronement in heaven. Nor is there anything about the believers' present relationship with Christ or their relationships with one another in Christ. To be sure, the writer's special concern is to oppose an idea about the Lord's coming that he regards as fundamentally wrong. But the fact remains that he does this without seeking in any way to place the *parousia* in a broader context. For Paul himself that context is the present experience of those who have been baptized into Christ's death. Like their faith and their love, their hope for the Lord's return derives from his continuing presence as the crucified and resurrected one.

In 2 Thessalonians, however, it is "the righteous judgment of God" (1:5), not God's love as disclosed in the cross, that sets the stage for the Lord's return. Certainly, believers can already experience "the eternal comfort and good hope" which derives from God's love and grace (2:16; see also 3:5, 16). But the writer's appeals are not based on who Christ has become for them, what he means for them now. They are based, rather, on what the Lord's return will mean: for those who have been faithful to the gospel, "glory" (2:14); and for those who have disobeyed, "eternal destruction" (1:9).

The Pastoral Epistles

There are good reasons to believe that these three letters (1, 2 Timothy and Titus) were written by the same person. But while they are in the form of letters to individuals, that is strictly a literary device. They are clearly intended for general use within the churches with which this writer is associated, perhaps somewhere in Asia Minor. The advice and appeals they offer are presented as the legacy that the venerable Paul is leaving for his younger followers (for example, 1 Tim 1:18; 4:11–12; 6:20a; 2 Tim 1:13–14; 2:1–2; Titus 2:15). Second Timothy has been given the special form of a "farewell" letter, written by the apostle in preparation for his martyr's death (2 Tim 4:6). We cannot be certain when these letters were actually written, although a date sometime in the first two decades of the second century seems likely.

Purpose and Character

Stated generally, and in this writer's own words, his purpose is to provide instructions about "how one ought to behave in the household of God, which is the church of the living God, the pillar and bulwark of the truth" (1 Tim 3:15). This aim derives from his concern about some kind of false teaching (1 Tim 1:3–4; 2 Tim 4:3–4; Titus 1:10–11) which he sees as a threat both to moral conduct and to ecclesiastical order.

It is not clear what the false doctrines were or by whom they were being promoted. There are hints that teachings about the resurrection (2 Tim 2:17b–18) and the law of Moses (1 Tim 1:6–11; Titus 3:9) were both involved, along with certain ascetic rules (1 Tim 4:1–5). However, our author seems not to be specifically concerned about false teachings concerning Christ. Thus, unlike Colossians and 2 Thessalonians, the christological affirmations in these letters stand pretty much on their own. They are not directly aimed at opposing views.

In the composition of these letters the writer has drawn heavily on traditional materials. Even more than the authors of the other deutero-Paulines, he relies on time-worn liturgical, creedal, hymnic, and ethical formulations. However, these traditions are subjected to neither interpretation nor exposition, nor are they used in the service of reasoned theological argumentation. Rather, they are simply *reasserted* as constituting what this writer regards as the apostolic norm. His Christian commitment does not include a commitment to theological reflection or debate. On the contrary, he expresses disdain for "meaningless talk" (1 Tim 1:6), "profane chatter" (1 Tim 6:20b; 2 Tim 2:16), "wrangling over words" (2 Tim 2:14), and the like (see also 1 Tim 1:6; 2 Tim 2:23). His own approach is exhibited in 1 Tim 6:3–4, where anyone who adheres to different teachings is denounced as "conceited, understanding nothing," and given to "a morbid craving for controversy and for disputes about words" (compare 2 Tim 2:16–19; 3:1–9; 4:15).

The Pauline legacy is evident throughout these letters, especially so in two of the passages which the author specifically identifies as traditional "sayings." The hymn-like affirmation of 2 Tim 2:11–13 includes the unmistakably Pauline conception of dying and rising with Christ (see Rom 6:5–8; 5:17):

[11]If we have died with him, we will also live with him; [12]if we endure, we will also reign with him . . .

In Titus 3:4–7 there is a similarly distinct echo of Paul's conception of justification (see Rom 3:21–28; 4:6; Gal 2:15–16):

[5][God] saved us, not because of any works of righteousness that we had done, but according to his mercy ... [7]so that, having been justified by his grace, we might become heirs according to the hope of eternal life.

Even in these passages, however, certain alterations of Paul's thought are evident. For instance, the apostle himself does not think of salvation as something already completed (note "saved" in 2 Tim 2:11), nor does he ever use the phrase "works of righteousness" (Titus 3:5). This author's view of the law's proper function also differs from Paul's. According to 1 Tim 1:8–10 the law has been given to prevent disobedience. Paul, however, believes that its proper role is to bring sin to life (Rom 7:7–11).

Examples like the ones just given could be multiplied. However, it is particularly important to observe that this writer is not very interested in Paul's teaching, not even in his teaching about Christ. He certainly has no interest at all in delineating or interpreting the apostle's thought. The writer's main concern is to offer Paul as the outstanding example of a true believer. To this end he portrays the apostle as a brave (2 Tim 2:8–10) but lonely martyr (2 Tim 4:6–8, 16), "suffering like a good soldier of Christ Jesus," just as every faithful Christian should (2 Tim 2:3, 10–14).

Affirmations about Christ

The word that best describes this author's religious point of view, including what he says about Christ, is *eclectic*. In writing these letters he has made use of very diverse concepts and traditions, both Christian and non-Christian. He has made no effort to harmonize these, even when they are in tension, or to integrate them into some larger theological conception.

Traditional statements are simply cited, when and as he thinks it appropriate. He seems to assume that his readers will find them meaningful just as they stand. Nor does he pause to reflect on how one concept may relate to another, or to worry that he sometimes uses key terms in different ways.

The eclectic and non-reflective character of the Pastorals becomes apparent as soon as one begins to survey the author's various christological affirmations. For example, the statement that "[God's] grace was given to us in Christ Jesus before the ages began" (2 Tim 1:9) implies the pre-existence of Christ. But that is not easily reconciled with the description of Christ as "a descendant of David" (2 Tim 2:8), which accords him messianic status. These are two distinct christological traditions.

Moreover, statements about the status and role of Christ are hardly distinguishable from statements about God. Indeed, a reference to "our great God and Savior, Jesus Christ" (Titus 2:13) seems to identify Christ *as* God, without qualification. We should not conclude from this, however, that our author has rejected other options and decided that this one alone is an adequate expression of Christ's status. Quite the opposite is the case. Elsewhere, other traditional formulations and statements have been used in which Christ is clearly distinguished from God, even though the two are still closely related. According to Titus 3:4–7, "God our Savior" has bestowed the Holy Spirit "through Jesus Christ our Savior." A particularly striking example is 1 Tim 2:5–6, where "Christ Jesus, himself human," is portrayed as the "one mediator between God and humankind." By the fourth century, certain of the church fathers were debating how Christ could be described as both "God" and "human." The author of the Pastorals gives no thought to such matters, however. In this case as in others, he allows two kinds of statements to stand side by side, unexplained.

Despite the reference to Christ's humanity, our author has

virtually nothing to say about Jesus' life on earth. His allusion to Jesus' trial before Pontius Pilate (1 Tim 6:13) is almost incidental. Moreover, like the other deutero-Paulinists he is quite silent about Jesus' teachings. His reference to "the sound words of our Lord Jesus Christ" (1 Tim 6:13) is not an exception. No particular saying of the earthly Jesus is in mind. As elsewhere (1 Tim 1:10; 2 Tim 1:13; 4:3; Titus 1:9), he is thinking of Christian teaching in general. In fact, the one saying that he cites from the Jesus tradition ("The laborer deserves to be paid," 1 Tim 5:18) he does not even attribute to Jesus (although Paul himself had; see the discussion of 1 Cor 9:14 – above, pp. 46–51). He simply appends it to a dictum that – like Paul in 1 Cor 9:9 – he identifies as scriptural.

Because this author's thought is so eclectic, it is difficult to identify one christological theme as dominant. It is not the saving death of Jesus, although that is affirmed (1 Tim 2:6; 2 Tim 2:14), nor is it his resurrection, although that is also in view (1 Tim 3:16; 2 Tim 2:8). What is most distinctive, even if not dominant, is the conception of Christ's "appearing." The Greek term used for this is *epiphaneia* (our author also uses the related verb), from which the church's season of "Epiphany" gets its name. As a religious term, already found in pre-Christian texts, it was used of a god's appearances within the course of history, ordinarily with some special manifestation of power. In 2 Thess 2:8 it had been used of Jesus' return at the *parousia* (NRSV: "the manifestation of his coming").

In the Pastorals, too, the term is applied to Jesus' expected return (1 Tim 6:14; 2 Tim 4:1, 8; Titus 2:13). His role as "the righteous judge" (2 Tim 4:8) is especially in view in these passages. Elsewhere, however, the same word is applied to Jesus' incarnation, to the *first* manifestation. According to 2 Tim 1:9–10 Christ's first appearing in history revealed the grace with which God had already entrusted the pre-existent Christ. Again in Titus 2:11 the incarnation is described as the manifestation of God's grace (using the related verb; compare Titus 3:4–7). In a sense, therefore, this concept of "epiphany" embraces the whole of Christ's saving work, as that is in view in the Pastorals. It looks back to his incarnation, and still farther back to his existence with God "before the ages began" (2 Tim 1:9–10). At the same time, it looks on ahead to Christ's eventual return in glory (Titus 2:13).

Concluding Observations

In the Pastoral Epistles no one image of Christ stands out above others. The author's concept of Christ's "appearing," though distinctive, encompasses several different images. In a way, his portrayal of Paul is executed more carefully and consistently than his portrayal of Christ. This is because the readers are to find in their martyred apostle the inspiration and model for their own faith and conduct as Christians.

Titus 2:11–14 can be singled out as an especially good example of the eclectic christology one finds in the Pastoral Epistles. This passage also shows how the writer's assertions about Christ are employed to support his moral exhortations.

[11]For the grace of God has appeared, bringing salvation to all, [12]training us to renounce impiety and worldly passions, and in the present age to live lives that are self-controlled, upright, and godly, [13]while we wait for the blessed hope and the manifestation of the glory of our great God and Savior, Jesus Christ. [14]He it is who gave himself for us that he might redeem us from all iniquity and purify for himself a people of his own who are zealous for good deeds.

Here the incarnation and *parousia* are both described as epiphanies (vv. 11, 13); salvation is attributed to God's grace as operative in Christ's atoning death (vv. 11, 14); and the present is viewed as a time for moral uprightness (vv. 12, 14) and hope (v. 13). How all of these are related is not spelled out. But the writer must think that they are, and wants his readers to think so, too.

Our author is not unique in having taken over diverse statements about Christ from the church's tradition. The same is true of Paul and of the other writers of the Pauline school. But in the apostle's own letters, and in each of the other deutero-Paulines, we have found one central christological image. The Jesus with whom Paul presents us is, especially, the crucified one. In Colossians Christ sits enthroned as the head of the cosmos. For the author of Ephesians he is, in particular, the head of the church. And in 2 Thessalonians Jesus is portrayed as the one who will return to execute the righteous judgment of God. From the eclecticism of the Pastoral Epistles, however, no one image has emerged. Perhaps that is just as well. Perhaps the varied christological affirmations of these letters can serve as a reminder that, from the beginning, Jesus' followers have had to look for many different ways to express his significance for their lives.

Suggested Reading and Discussion Questions

1 From Jesus to Paul

The life and faith of the earliest Christians in Jerusalem can be reconstructed only with great difficulty. Three rather different, but representative attempts may be found in Hans Conzelmann's *History of Primitive Christianity*, tr. by John E. Steely (Nashville and New York: Abingdon, 1973), Leonhard Goppelt's *Apostolic and Post-Apostolic Times*, tr. by Robert A. Guelich (New York and Evanston: Harper Torchbook, 1970), and Gerd Theissen's *Sociology of Early Palestinian Christianity*, tr. by John Bowden (Philadelphia: Fortress, 1978). More specifically focused on the relation of the church's faith to Jesus' own ministry is Willi Marxsen's *Jesus and Easter: Did God Raise the Historical Jesus from the Dead?*, tr. by Victor Paul Furnish (Nashville: Abingdon, 1990). Alan Segal offers a Jewish historian's view of Paul's conversion in his provocative book, *Paul the Convert: The Apostolate and Apostasy of Saul the Pharisee* (New Haven and London: Yale University Press, 1990). An excellent, comprehensive introduction to Paul's life and ministry is Jürgen Becker's *Paul*, tr. by O. C. Dean, Jr. (Louisville: Westminster/John Knox, 1993). For a more specialized study, see Martin Hengel's *The Pre-Christian Paul*, tr. by John Bowden (Philadelphia: Trinity Press International, 1991).

1. Compare what Acts says about Paul's pre-Christian life and conversion with what can be learned about these from Paul's own letters. What accounts for the differences?

What does this situation require of those who wish to understand Paul?

2. Why is it misleading to speak of Paul's "conversion" to Christianity? What factors played a role in changing him from a persecutor of the church into an apostle of Christ?

3. Why do most scholars think it unlikely that Paul had ever come into contact with Jesus during his earthly ministry? If Paul had been acquainted with Jesus, do you suppose that would have caused him to write differently about Jesus? If so, in what respects?

2 Paul's Knowledge about Jesus and
3 Sayings of Jesus in Paul's Gospel

Discussions of Paul's knowledge about Jesus, and of his use of sayings attributed to Jesus, are confined largely to scholarly monographs and articles. One of the more readable, general studies is Marinus de Jonge's *Christology in Context: The Earliest Christian Response to Jesus* (Philadelphia: Westminster, 1988). The Introduction and Part I are especially relevant for the question of Paul and Jesus. Readers who wish to pursue the specific topics of chapters 2 and 3 in greater depth will find more specialized studies in the following volumes: Nils A. Dahl, *Jesus the Christ. The Historical Origins of Christological Doctrine*, ed. by Donald H. Juel (Minneapolis: Fortress, 1991); David Wenham (ed.), *The Jesus Tradition Outside the Gospels* (Gospel Perspectives, vol. V; Sheffield: JSOT Press, 1985); A. J. M. Wedderburn (ed.), *Paul and Jesus. Collected Essays* (Journal for the Study of the New Testament Supplements, vol. 37; Sheffield: JSOT Press, 1989).

1. A once-popular view was that Paul turned "the religion of Jesus" into "a religion about Jesus," and thus became "the second founder of Christianity." Why does Paul's reliance on traditions about Jesus undercut this notion?

2. How can an awareness of specific traditions used by Paul help one better understand the apostle's own point of view about Jesus?

3. Reflect on the observations offered in the concluding section of chapter 3. Do you believe they are valid? What questions do they raise for you? Have you any observations to add about Paul's use of the sayings attributed to Jesus?

4 Jesus in Paul's Gospel

Paul's gospel has been the subject of many important studies. Among the more recent, general discussions, the following are representative: J. Christiaan Beker, *The Triumph of God: The Essence of Paul's Thought*, tr. by Loren T. Stuckenbruck (Philadelphia: Fortress, 1990), a "mainline" Protestant interpretation; Joseph A. Fitzmyer, S.J., *Paul and His Theology. A Brief Sketch* (2nd edn.; Englewood Cliffs: Prentice-Hall, 1989), an important contribution by a Roman Catholic interpreter; Ralph P. Martin, *Reconciliation. A Study of Paul's Theology* (Atlanta: John Knox Press, 1980), an "evangelical" Protestant approach; and Herman Ridderbos, *Paul: An Outline of His Theology*, tr. by Richard De Witt (Grand Rapids: Eerdmans, 1975), in the Calvinist tradition.

More specifically focused on Paul's view of Jesus are Charles B. Cousar's *A Theology of the Cross. The Death of Jesus in the Pauline Letters* (Overtures to Biblical Theology; Minneapolis: Fortress, 1990), and Robin Scroggs's *Christology in Paul and John* (Proclamation Commentaries; Philadelphia: Fortress, 1988). A very different approach is taken by the noted liberationist theologian, Juan Luis Segundo, in *The Humanist Christology of Paul* (Jesus of Nazareth Yesterday and Today, vol. III; Maryknoll: Orbis, 1986). Paul's understanding of Christian community is explored in Robert Banks', *Paul's Idea of Community: The Early House Churches in their Historical*

Setting (Grand Rapids: Eerdmans, 1980), and in J. Paul Sampley's *Pauline Partnership in Christ. Christian Community and Commitment in Light of Roman Law* (Philadelphia: Fortress, 1980).

1. Three important Pauline terms are *righteousness*, *reconciliation*, and *redemption*. How do these terms overlap in meaning? What does each of them suggest about Paul's understanding of Jesus? In what respect is each distinctive?

2. Choose one of the shorter Pauline letters (Galatians, Philippians, or 1 Thessalonians), and study it carefully for what is said or implied there about (a) Jesus and (b) the community of faith. What correlations do you find between the apostle's statements concerning (a) and (b)?

3. In what ways is Paul's understanding of Jesus related to his interpretation of Christian baptism, of the Lord's Supper, and of "the good life"?

5 Jesus According to the "Pauline School"

Good introductions to and commentaries on the writings discussed in this chapter can be found in *Harper's Bible Commentary* (James L. Mays, General Editor; San Francisco: Harper & Row, 1988). A book by Raymond F. Collins, *Letters That Paul Did Not Write. The Epistle to the Hebrews and The Pauline Pseudepigrapha* (Good News Studies, 28; Wilmington: Michael Glazier, 1988), focuses on the themes of these writings, including the topic of christology. Collins also provides a useful bibliography (pp. 273–308). One short chapter of M. de Jonge's book on New Testament christology (listed above for chapters 2 and 3) is devoted to the deutero-Paulines (pp. 124–29); and in J. Christiaan Beker's *Heirs of Paul: Paul's Legacy in the New Testament and in the Church Today* (Minneapolis: Fortress, 1991), chapters 3 and 4 are especially to the point (pp. 35–97).

1. Check for yourself the suggestions made in this chapter about the central christological images in Colossians, Ephesians, and 2 Thessalonians, respectively. Read each letter through asking yourself the question, "How is Christ being presented to me?" What are your own conclusions? Which of these presentations do you find most meaningful, and why?

2. Drawing from all six letters of the Pauline school, assemble the passages which most directly affirm the saving significance of Jesus' death. Compare these with one another, looking both at the ways they are similar and the ways in which they differ.

3. First Timothy 3:16, like Col 1:15–20, is sometimes identified as a christological hymn. Compare these two passages with one another, and then also with the Christ hymn in Phil 2:6–11. Note how these three affirmations are alike and how they are different. What is distinctive about each? Is it possible to say that one or the other of them is a more adequate summary of Jesus' significance? If so, which one(s) and why? If not, why not?

Index of Subjects and Names

Index of Passages

Other Ancient Writings